YOUR PERSONALITY IN HANDWRITING

BY LYN BROOK

EMBASSY BOOKS

www.embassybooks.in

YOUR PERSONALITY IN HANDWRITING

by Lyn Book

Published in India by :

EMBASSY BOOK DISTRIBUTORS
120, Great Western Building,
Maharashtra Chamber of Commerce Lane,
Kala Ghoda, Fort,
Mumbai- 400 023.
Tel : (+91-22) 22819546 / 32967415
Email : info@embassybooks.in
www.embassybooks.in

CONTENTS

FOREWORD

When I was asked to examine the manuscript for this book I approached the task with keen interest, for the reason that in bringing this subject to the fore the author performs a good service. While handwriting analysis is used as a supplemental diagnostic tool in the field of psychological testing, the purpose of this book is to acquaint the non-professional person with the functioning of graphology and the way it can help him to understand his own basic personality, as well as to give an insight into those in whom he is interested. The book also tells the reader the analytical methods by which a professional graphologist is able to discover fundamental potential abilities in a handwriting which could serve as a guide for the better application of them.

Graphology is neither guesswork nor prediction. It is a serious study of the way in which the writer expresses his individuality by the hundreds of indications shown in the handwriting, such as the size of the small and capital letters, the pressure, spacing, margins, and dozens of other signs which must first be considered separately and then put together to produce the sum total of the personality picture. While intuition on the part of the analyst plays some part in this work (just as it is well for anyone who works with people to have intuition) the conclusive analysis of a handwriting depends on practical application of the theories of graphology to the work. Too often the layman will look at a specimen of handwriting and say "My intuition tells me this writer is a salesman . . ." whereas the professional graphologist knows this is a probable guess but not always a sure one; the handwriting analyst does not "guess" even though the keenness of intuition may respond to that particular writing and recognize it to be an outgoing personality which might fit into sales work.

The graphologist does not base an analysis merely on the separate formations or signs in the writing; what a crossing of the letter "t" or the dotting of an "i" may signify in one handwriting may not hold true in another person's writing. The way the indications in the specimen of handwriting relate to one another is the process by which the careful analysis should be made. Therefore, while the separate meanings of individual signs are given in this book, the reader must not be led into the easy and often erroneous path of trying to determine a person's fundamental character simply by one or two formations which are prominent in the handwriting. It is well to bear in mind, too, that in the printing of this book the reproductions of the specimens of handwriting may not show the actual pressure and connections of the lines of writing as clearly as in the originals.

An amusing question is usually put to the graphologist: "Why can't I change my handwriting so that it will contain all the superlative traits which are discussed in a book on handwriting analysis? Won't you then be fooled?" The answer to that is a flat "NO" because handwriting is an instinctive gesture of the inner personality; the harder a person tries to imitate a style of handwriting the more "phoney" it will appear, and immediately the graphologist has the first clue to the falseness of the handwriting and proceeds to make the analysis "between the phoney lines." Nobody, by consciously trying to change to a style or type of penmanship, changes his fundamental personality — and that will come out regardless of how cleverly the writer may think he has fooled the graphologist.

This book gives a fine insight into the meaning and function of graphology. But the amateur graphologist must be warned that just reading one book on the subject does not make him an expert handwriting analyst! The subject cannot be absorbed hastily or flippantly; it requires long and serious study if one is to become a professional in the field.

Dorothy Sara
Past President,
American Graphohgical Society
New York, 1960

Chapter 1

WHAT IS GRAPHOLOGY?

Graphology is the study of the formations of handwriting to diagnose the personality traits. It is not concerned with any particular style of penmanship; the analysis is not based on whether the handwriting is "beautiful" or "ugly" and does not recognize any such designation. Graphology studies each handwriting individually and not as belonging to a certain "type." The handwriting analyst examines each handwriting in the same way a fingerprint expert does his work, realizing that each person has his or her own unique characteristics.

A graphologist is not to be confused with a "handwriting expert." The latter does not analyze handwriting with the purpose of determining the personality; the expert looks for marks of identification in establishing the authenticity of questioned documents, or to find the culprit in the cases of anonymous letters, etc. This does not mean that the graphologist may not also be an identification expert, or that the expert may not know how to analyze a handwriting; but usually the two professions are distinct from each other in the performance of their work.

According to researchers in historical background of the subject of graphology, references are found as far back as the second century A. D. when C. Suetonius Tranquillus mentioned that he found some strangeness in Augustus Caesar's handwriting. Then in the eleventh century some learned Chinese recognized a relationship between the formations of their writing with the personalities of the writers. There may have been scholars in Europe in earlier times who also saw this relationship, but written work does not appear on this except some reference to Nero who stated in a letter that he judged one of his courtiers to be treacherous because of his handwriting.

In the early seventeenth century Camillo Baldo, an Italian scholar, wrote a treatise in which he set down specific rules to follow in making an anaylsis of handwriting. In the next century essays were written by scholars in Switzerland, Germany and England, discussing the use of handwriting analysis as an understanding of personality.

It was in the nineteenth century that Baldo's treatise became the subject of interest to a French churchman, the Abbè Flandrin, who held group discussions with other scholars on this method of personality analysis, and he published a manual which was more fully developed than the original set of rules written by Camillo Baldo. It was the Abbè Flandrin who coined a name for this new science — graphology — by combining the Greek words, *grapho* (meaning "to write") and *ology* ("science").

An apt pupil of Flandrin, the Abb'e Michon, is often said to be the originator of the term "graphology," and it may be they both collaborated on it. It is not of great import, but the matter is mentioned so that credit is given to both the teacher and his pupil. Michon proved himself a scientific student of the subject and in 1872 he wrote his book *Mystère de Yècriture* which was a contribution to the growing literature and knowledge of graphology. Following Michon was his pupil, Crèpieux-Jamin, who added to his teacher's work in classifying individual traits disclosed in handwritings.

During the eighteenth and nineteenth centuries many intellectuals formed study circles for the discussion of handwriting analysis or pursued the subject on their own, and they helped to spark interest in this science. Among these were such individuals as Edgar Allen Poe, Disraeli, Johann von Goethe, Madame de Staèl, Robert Browning, Sir Walter Scott, Thomas Gainsborough, and others.

In the late nineteenth and the early twentieth centuries much scholarly work in the development of graphology was done in Germany. We find among them the names of academic scientists, such as G. Meyer, H. H. Busse, W. Preyer, and G. Schneidemühl. Around the year 1910 Dr. Ludwig Klages, a scholar in the fields of psychology and philosophy, did excellent work in proving the principles of graphology and he set the standards of its application in relation to the broader aspects of his work. Dr. Klages is looked upon as "the father of modern graphology" by those in the professional field of handwriting analysis.

Dr. Max Pulver, a university professor in Switzerland, worked on the evaluation of symbolic aspects in handwriting as a further development of the work done by Klages. He, Pulver, showed the relationship between the handwriting symbols and their interpretation of dreams in the theory of psychoanalysis.

In this country graphology was little known until about fifty years ago when Louise Rice, a woman who was active in the writing field and had a pioneering spirit, brought handwriting analysis to the attention of the American public. There is hardly a professional handwriting analyst in this country today who was not influenced by her and who does not look upon the late Louise Rice as the "mother of graphology" in the United States. She spearheaded the formation of The American Graphological Society in 1927, which today is an active organization throughout the United States and Canada, with headquarters in the city of New York. Its membership consists of professional handwriting analysts and students of graphology, as well as physicians, psychologists, writers, educators, and others interested in analysis of personalities.

Many names of scientists and many other references to their work in the field of handwriting analysis could be included in the telling of the background of graphology; but the foregoing should prove sufficient in this small book to show that graphology is certainly not an intuitive "guesswork" method of analysis but is based on sound principles of procedure.

Handwriting is an instinctive gesture; the late Dr. Wemer Wolff (a psychology professor) said that writing was a personal expression, "... a bodily movement registered graphically." Handwriting is as much an instinctive individual expression as the way a person talks or walks or uses his hands. No matter how a child is taught to write, when he becomes an adult he may make many unconscious changes in the formations of the letters, in the size and pressure of the writing. Take thirty children in one class in school, all taught by the same rules of penmanship; but ten or fifteen or twenty years later each one will undoubtedly have some individual way of writing, and in some cases hardly a trace of the original style of writing remains. Of course some adults do not alter their handwritings from the first day they were taught to write! But the purpose of this paragraph is to point out that each person writes in a manner that is unconsciously expressive of his or her individual personality. And it is this phase of handwriting that concerns the graphologist rather than the styles or rules of penmanship laid down by the teacher in the first grade.

In line with discussing what graphology is, a few stock questions usually arise:

1.   What type of person asks for an analysis?

2.   What is the usual reason for anyone to want an analysis?

3.   What result is gained once a handwriting is analyzed?

The answers to the foregoing are:

1.   Graphology applies universally, to men and women, from teen-age to old age; requests for analyses come from people of all social and financial and intellectual areas.

2.   It is impossible to state one reason; there are as many motives for requesting an analysis as there are human activities and problems. Some parents send their children's handwritings to be studied by the graphologist because they would like to know the potential abilities in order to guide their offspring to suitable schooling or vocational training. In some cases a man meets a girl and wants to know about her, so he sends her letter to the graphologist. In reverse, a girl meets a man and wants the graphologist to let her know what kind of person he is after she re ceives her first note from him. Or a firm wants to hire a salesman or a secretary, so the letter of application is forwarded to the graphologist for a "personality picture" of the prospective employee. And sometimes an employee may send the handwriting of the head of his firm in order to understand him better. The "in-laws" situation often makes use of the handwriting analyst, too, when parents want to find out about their prospective daughter- or son-in-law. Of course not in every case is it the handwriting of another person; in many instances a man or woman wants to know whether he or she is fitted for a certain career, or is interested in having the graphologist point out the basic traits in order to have better self-understanding.

4

3.   Actually the best result is that a person gets a clearer understanding of the fundamental elements of his own personality make-up; or, in sending another person's handwriting, he finds out about the inner personality that exists there. This certainly leads to better human relationships when one is aware of the basic traits and can then adapt to them in an intelligent manner. It helps people to realize that a trait which they may think is just a superficial one and could be eliminated in themselves or someone else, may actually be something that is innate and which one must learn to accept and then adapt to the situation.

Graphology is not concerned with the "outer" person; its function is to find the "inner" personality. No claims are made that graphology will change anyone; all the handwriting analyst can do is to tell what the writing reveals and then it is up to the one who receives the analysis to benefit by a clearer understanding of himself and others.

Graphology has a definite place in personality testing; it is of valuable use in the fields of psychology, personnel selection, and other aspects of personal counseling. Research is going on in the relationship of graphology and the diagnosis of physical and mental diseases; tests are also being made in the field of hypnosis to study the handwritings of people when consciously awake and when in hypnotic sleep. But these are matters for the clinical worker and are not part of the study of the layman.

Your Personality in Handwriting

Chapter 2

WHAT GRAPHOLOGY CANNOT REVEAL

Before telling what graphology can reveal through the study of handwriting formations, it is well to point out what it cannot reveal. The professional handwriting analyst usually specifies these facts to his clients, to dispel any misconceptions as to what can be disclosed in the writing.

The sex of the writer is not seen; fundamentally there is no difference in the male or female handwriting, so if the specimen is not signed with a full name which designates the sex, the graphologist should be told if the writing is from a man or a woman. Sometimes a signature is a nickname which doesn't signify the sex; or there are some names which are used by both men and women, such as Jean, Pat, Ronnie, etc. Or a client may send a sample of writing and say "This is from my friend" without specifying whether it's a boy-friend or girl-friend.

Age is not disclosed in the handwriting; the graphologist will discover if the person is intellectually and emotionally mature or immature, but cannot know the chronological

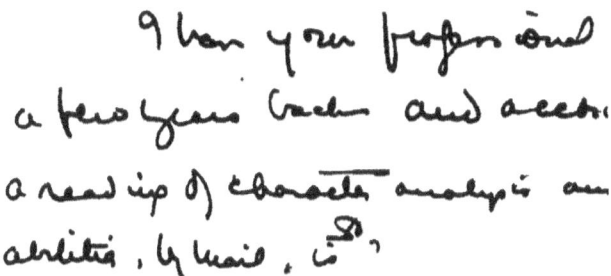

ILLUSTRATION NO. 1

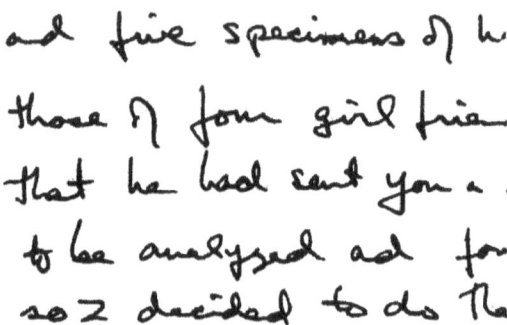

ILLUSTRATION NO. 2

age. Someone at the age of sixty might have the naive sentimentality and mentality of a teen-ager, and the handwriting will appear to be that of a young person. Or a young school girl might have a highly developed intellectual mind, and her writing will appear to be that of a much older person. It is, therefore, much fairer to the subject of the analysis if the handwriting analyst is told the age. The actual date of birth is not necessary, as that has nothing to do with an analysis of handwriting; just the approximate age is sufficient.

As an example of neither sex nor age being discernible in handwriting, here are four illustrations of writing received by me.

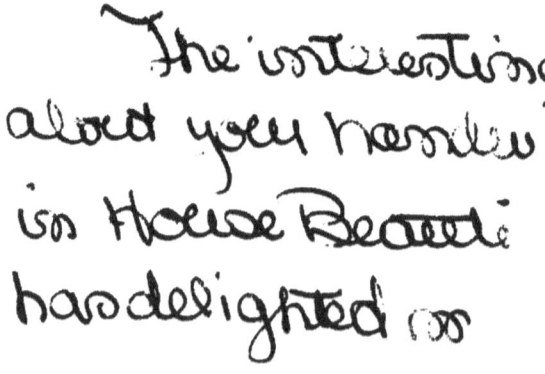

ILLUSTRATION NO. 3

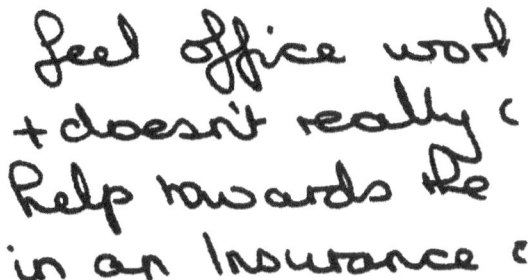

ILLUSTRATION NO. 4

Specimens 1 and 2 are quite similar and show they have most traits in common; yet No. 1 is written by a woman in her fifties and No. 2 by a man of twenty-two.

Specimens 3 and 4 show similarities of traits and both are written by women; but No. 3 is the age of twenty-six and No. 4 in her late forties.

Incidentally, while on the subject of age, a graphologist will often be asked how old a child should be before an analysis can be made of the handwriting. This is not an answerable query, because in one child the writing at the age of six might lend itself well to analysis, whereas another child's handwriting at the age of ten might not yet prove an adequate subject for the graphologist's study. So there is no definite minimum age at which the writing of a child should be submitted for analysis. This depends entirely on the individual development of each child.

Whether a person is married or single is not seen in the handwriting; marriage doesn't really change the fundamental personality traits although in some cases it might enhance or minimize some of them dependent on the situations in that marriage. Therefore, if a female signature does not say "Miss" or "Mrs." the graphologist has no way of knowing if she is married. Of course, the "Mr." preceding a man's name is ambiguous, and he may be either single or married. Thus, if the analysis in any way is expected to touch upon the marital state, the graphologist should be told the subject's status. Referring back to the illustrations, Nos. 2 and 3 are from unmarried people; Nos. 1 and 4 are married; but there is absolutely nothing in any of these specimens to indicate their state of single- or double-blessedness.

A common incident in the course of the day's work for the graphologist is to receive the handwriting of a man and a woman, and to be asked if the two will make a compatible marriage. This is certainly not possible to tell as it would be in the realm of guesswork or prediction, neither of which has the slightest relationship to graphology. The clients are told that even when two handwritings fundamentally have a good deal in common, there is no way of knowing how the marriage will turn out because success is sometimes dependent on influences outside of their own personalities, such as in-laws, finances, having to move to another area, careers, and so on. On the other hand, two handwritings may be full of traits contradictory to each other; yet if both people are intelligent and if outside influences are good, they may reach a most comfortable and compatible marriage. The only function the graphologist can perform is to tell, according to the study of both handwritings, the basic personalities of the man and the woman, and from then on it's up to the two of them to understand their own selves and each other and to happily produce an intelligent marriage.

The handwriting cannot reveal whether a person is a parent; having children doesn't alter the basic traits of personality of a mother or father. Therefore, if the analysis is desired to touch upon a parent-child relationship, it is necessary to tell the graphologist if the writer has children.

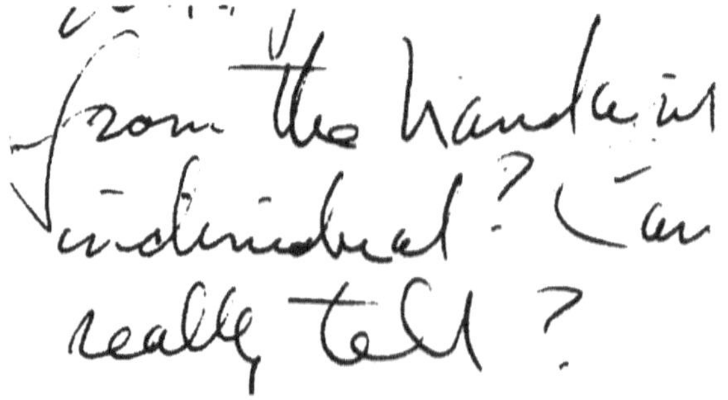

ILLUSTRATION NO. 5

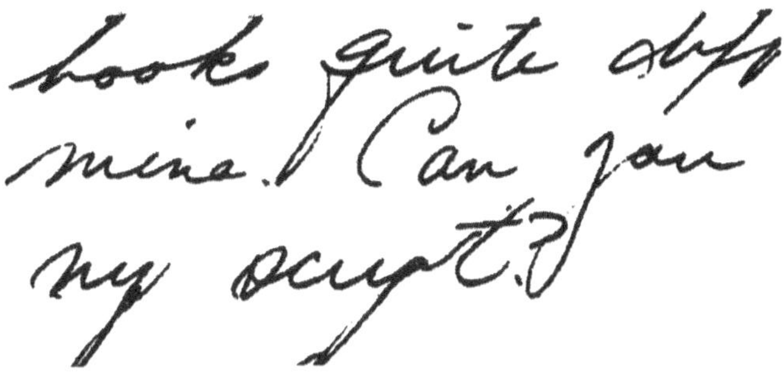

ILLUSTRATION NO. 6

Members of one family don't have a "family handwriting" nor for that matter do identical twins necessarily write alike. The two specimens (Nos. 5 and 6) shown here belong to a pair of adult twin brothers. While there are some similarities — for instance, the same capital letter "C" — this is an example to show how two brothers, so closely associated, write differently.

Each person in a family is a distinct individual, and each one has his or her own handwriting. A graphologist is often asked to "pick out which handwritings are of one family." But that is impossible. If some of them do write alike it is a coincidence; of course what may seem to be "alike" to the layman may not be so to the professional graphologist who may find many differences through analysis, even though on the surface and at quick glance the handwritings appear to be similar.

The work or hobby in which a person is engaged cannot be seen by the graphologist, because there is no such things as a "secretary's handwriting" or a "mechanic's handwriting" or the writing of any kind of activity one does. For instance, while potential abilities seen in a dozen girls' handwritings indicate they are all suited to secretarial work, each one has her own personality traits. Even though all could be efficient secretaries, one is affectionate and another is aloof, one girl is generous while others are more cautious. For that reason, when a client writes, "I am not happy in my job," or "Do you think I am suited to the job I am going to undertake?", if she or he doesn't tell what the job is, the graphologist cannot guess it and so cannot be of specific aid. Many people are successfully engaged in work or avocational activities which may not show in the handwriting as potential abilities. If a person is intelligent and efficient he may be able to perform work because of resourcefulness in adapting to a situation, even if the handwriting doesn't point to that particular work. Therefore, it is best to know the specific job or the profession in which a person is engaged or wants to do, before proceeding with the analysis.

As an example of the difference in the handwritings of five men in the same field, here are the signatures of Tolstoy, Dreiser, Zola, Stevenson, and Wilde, the distinguished authors. The individualistic personality of each man is expressed in his handwriting; they are not alike even though the five were engaged in the art and profession of writing about the same period of time.

ILLUSTRATIONS NOS. 7, 8, 9, 10 AND 11

Whether a person has gone to schools of higher learning or has acquired his knowledge on his own, cannot be seen in the handwriting. The analysis tells if the writer has an intellectual quality of mind or if the intelligence is the sound common-sense kind without being scholarly; but as graphology is not guess work the analyst cannot know if the education is based on formal schooling or if the person is self-taught.

Often a graphologist is asked, "How can I get along better with my co-workers?" or some similar reference to another person or group. Unless the handwritings of the others are included the analyst is unable to tell anything about the relationship between them and the one who asks such a question. In order to know how some people may find an understanding of one another, it is necessary to see the handwriting of each person concerned rather than to have a one-sided picture by analyzing only one specimen of writing.

The nationality (where a person was born) is not disclosed in the handwriting. Of course there are variations in the styles of writing of different countries, such as the Germans using a more angular form than the Latin script (which includes the American, English, French, Spanish and other handwritings), the British writing is generally simple in its formations, the Italian and Spanish scripts are usually graceful and have some flourishes, the Russian writing is generally large and flowing as is the usual American script. This does not mean that all people in one country write alike specifically even though they may follow a certain style generally. In America during the past few years the manuscript (block printing) manner of writing has been used in many schools, which adds another "national" handwriting. The question then arises, "If there is such a thing as a national handwriting, why can't a graphologist know where a person was born?" and the way to answer that is to cite a case where a person born in Germany is brought to America in early childhood and attends an American school; his handwriting then is typical of that taught in this country and not where he was born. Or, a person born in the United States is sent abroad to attend a school in France; when he returns he undoubtedly writes in the French style of penmanship and not in the way the American child writes. The graphologist sees, in the "national" style of writing, the influence of

13

the teacher during the child's penmanship-learning years rather than the actual place of birth.

When the left hand is used for writing it may not be distinguishable as such to the handwriting analyst. It is a good idea to state if the handwriting is left-handed when submitting a specimen of it for analysis; there is no essential difference in the traits shown in the writing, but the graphologist may find it necessary to make some allowances for the degree of a forward or backhand slant of writing because of its being done with the left hand.

A graphologist can do a general analysis of a sample of handwriting without being told the sex, age, marital status, work, nationality, or if left-handed writing. But it is best if these details are submitted in addition to the specimen of writing, so that the graphologist may be more specific in the analysis and thus be of greater service to the client.

Chapter 3

LEGIBILITY AND ILLEGIBILITY

A common tendency is to look at a handwriting and form a fast impression of the personality from the appearance of the script. The writing may present a beautiful picture on the sheet of paper through its legibility, and the reaction is one of pleasantness; or it may be so illegible that the reaction is adverse.

In some cases the reaction may be correct, but the chances are that in most instances it may be wrong. There is no guarantee that a so-called beautiful handwriting means a highly developed mind or sweet character, any more than it means that an illegible handwriting belongs to a person whose mind is not too bright and whose character traits are on that same low level. The graphologist truly "reads between the lines" of the handwriting, and discovers the causes which produce its ultimate clear or confusing appearance.

The age of the writer is important; a child just learning to write usually produces legible formations because the attention is directed toward that end. Adults who love to work with details and are meticulous with them also form their letters legibly. In an adult, however, the legibility has a freer flow than the child's.

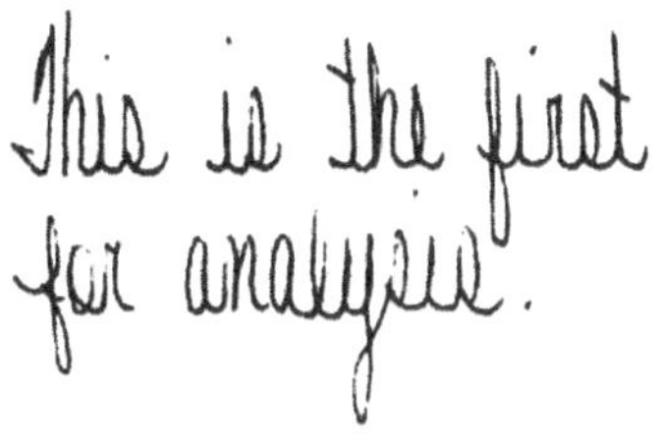

ILLUSTRATION NO. 12

This is the writing of a boy in the fourth grade; it is still labored and shows he is conscious of the legible way in which he forms his letters. But it also reveals he has a mind that is interested in details, that all his work is done in a methodical manner. This boy is never impulsive; he proceeds with care in all that he undertakes.

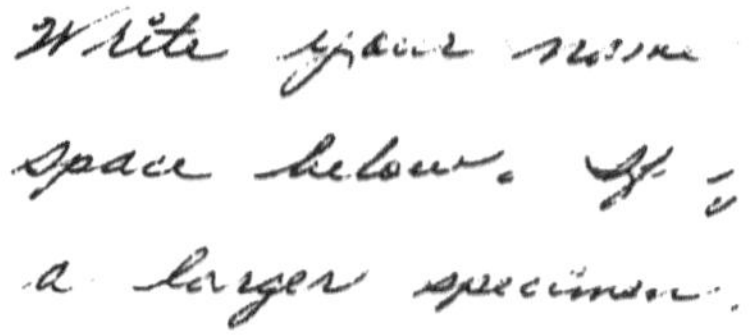

ILLUSTRATION NO. 13

This legible specimen of moderate-size writing was done by a woman of twenty-nine. Notice that it is not as restrained as the writing of the boy. While her mind is interested in and careful with details, it is also much freer and she is more self-confident. A sense of beauty is seen in this writing, with its graceful rhythmic forward movement and the circle "i" dot; but these signs will be discussed in later chapters. The purpose of showing it here is to call attention to the legibility in an adult's handwriting.

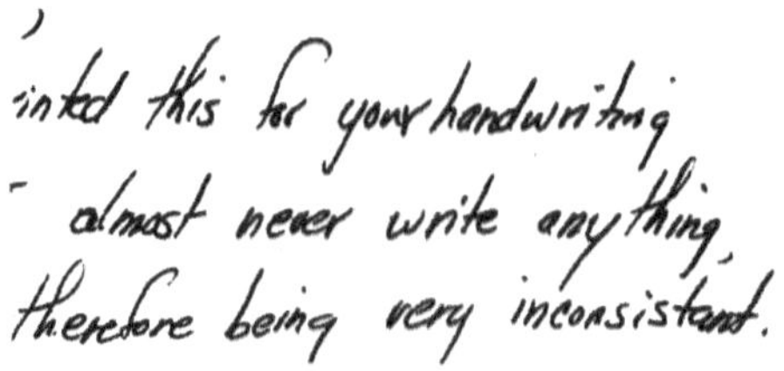

ILLUSTRATION NO. 14

This writing becomes "printing" and when you see a legible script which has a combination of cursive and printed formations it's a sign of a constructive mind. This was done by a man of thirty-five who is an architect. The legibility of his writing shows the clarity of thought, and the printed formations reveal resourcefulness of mind in tackling new ideas.

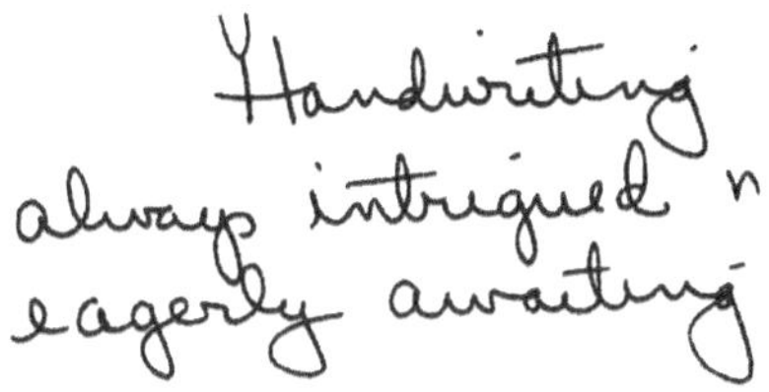

ILLUSTRATION NO. 15

Large legible writing discloses a combination of sociability (shown in large formations) plus practicality (the legibility which indicates application to details). This specimen is from a woman in her young thirties, who is a secretary. The job is well-suited to her as it involves meeting people and at the same time she performs the details of her work in a careful manner.

Apart from whatever other individual meanings are seen in the other signs it contains, the general summation of a legible handwriting is that it reveals a desire to do all work with accuracy, a mind that functions best when it is fully acquainted with each separate detail of a plan, a hesitancy to proceed with a spontaneous reaction, and a tendency to conform to whatever is the accepted pattern in his or her area of social and work activities. But this is a general statement and each individual's handwriting must be studied in relation to the other specific signs indicated.

Now we come to illegible writers. There cannot be any one cause why a person writes illegibly; it is essential to study all phases of the handwriting to find the reason therefor. In some cases illegibility may be caused by little or no education, or by a confused and easily irritated mind, or by lack of emotional discipline. This is usually seen in a handwriting that does not have any outstanding original formations, but is just an ordinary script which is written carelessly, has a disordered appearance and is hard to read.

However, there is the other extreme where the illegibility may be the result of a brilliant and individualistic mind belonging to a person who is a non-conformist and does not feel the need to make easily-read letter formations. In fact, often such a person takes a pride in his or her independence in not writing like everybody else does. Following are three illustrations which appear to be illegible at first quick glance, yet are easy to read once the eye recognizes the "pattern" in the writing; this is often referred to as cryptic handwriting by graphologists.

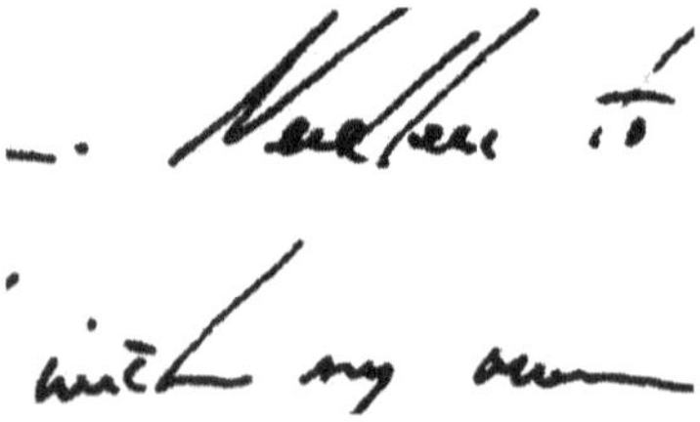

ILLUSTRATION NO. 16

ILLUSTRATION NO. 17

ILLUSTRATION NO. 17

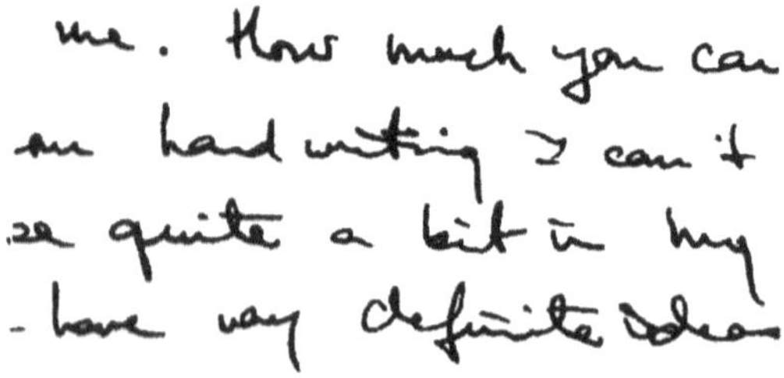

ILLUSTRATION NO. 18

These are all written by men. Nos. 16 and 17 are in their forties; the former is a designer of stage sets, the latter a designer of tools. No. 18 is a twenty-two year old senior in college who aims to pursue a career in creative writing.

An illegible handwriting is often used by the diplomat, the one who does not want to divulge any more to others than he or she feels they are entitled to know. This is shown in specimen No. 16 in which you will notice the words taper down at the end, which is a sign of the secretive person.

Sometimes an over-abundant use of punctuation marks gives a cluttered and hard-to-read appearance to a handwriting that actually has legible formations. Too frequent substitution of long dashes (or a group of short dashes or dots) in place of commas and periods, and exclamation points placed at end and even in middle of sentences, and lavish use of quotation marks and underlining of words, all indicate a most vivid imagination. The writer dramatizes every little thing and is often carried away by enthusiasms to a point of unreality, and finds it difficult to concentrate too long on one idea or activity. Such a personality is not easy to understand, but is generally most interesting to others.

Your Personality in Handwriting

Chapter 4

MARGINS

Margins are like a frame setting off the writing on a sheet of paper; they have special significance in showing the artistic taste of the writer as well as the attitude about spending or saving money. For this reason, in order to get a true analysis, it is best to see a specimen of handwriting done on paper which does not have ruled or printed margins. When writing is done on a small card or in a little address book it does not show the natural margins which the writer might make on a normal letter-size sheet. Therefore, when an analysis is made of the handwriting crowded onto a small card or sheet, or on paper with ruled margins, the analyst takes this into consideration and makes allowances for same.

When the four margins (the left and the right, as well as at the top and bottom of the sheet) are wide all around we deduce that the writer has an artistic appreciation; he may or may not be able to do any work in art but he has good taste in it. And the wider the margins the more inclined is the person to spend money to acquire the beautiful things he admires.

This does not mean that the person who makes narrow margins does not have an artistic appreciation, but it shows that he is more careful about spending money to get the fine things he admires.

When a writer makes no margins at all, either to the left or the right, it is indeed the sign of a frugal person who shows great practicality in using up every sixteenth-of-an-inch of the paper and not wasting any of it in "plain white space."

The following specimens are for the purpose of showing variations in the left-side margin:

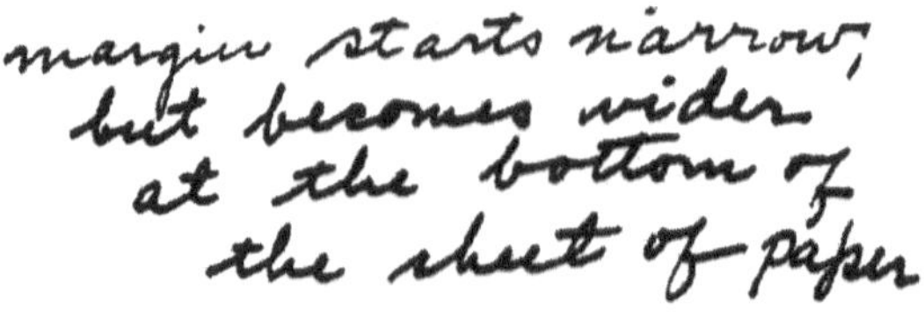

margin starts narrow, but becomes wider at the bottom of the sheet of paper

ILLUSTRATION NO. 19

The narrow left-side margin at the top of the sheet indicates a realization of the practical aspects of being thrifty, but the margin becomes wider as it goes down the sheet and so we know that this writer's good taste and unconscious generosity overcomes the conscious desire to save. This person often experiences an inner struggle trying to adjust the mind to stick to a budget, whereas the generous heart usually wins out.

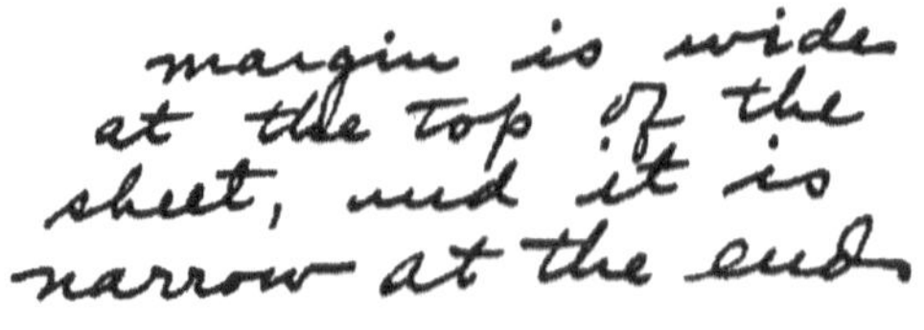

margin is wide at the top of the sheet, and it is narrow at the end

ILLUSTRATION NO. 20

But when the reverse occurs in the handwriting, with the left-side margin starting with a wide space and then tapering down to narrowness as it gets to the bottom of the sheet, we find that the conscious gesture of being a spender is held in check and the unconscious thrifty nature is able to keep any wastefulness in check.

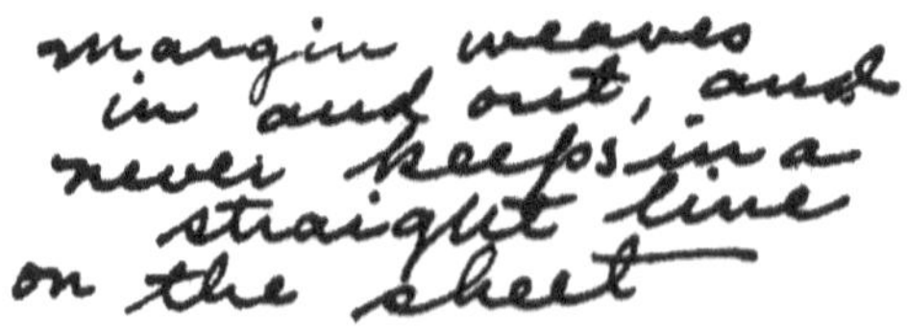

margin weaves in and out, and never keeps in a straight line on the sheet

ILLUSTRATION NO. 21

The left-side margin which is changeably wide and narrow and never kept to an orderly line discloses an erratic sense of finance, and there is often poor judgment in taste and in selecting things of beauty and artistic value. Such a writer is generous and thrifty in spurts, and usually the "penny wise, pound foolish" compulsive spender.

The margin at the right of the sheet is not so important as the left-side margin; however, it helps to emphasize some of the points of saving or spending. In studying the right-side margin it must be taken into consideration that sometimes a person does not leave any margin at the right because consciously he doesn't want to stop to hyphenate a long word, or because the mind rushes so swiftly that he reaches the edge of the sheet before he realizes it. But, generally, this is what may be gleaned from an examination of the right-side margin:

When the left-side margin is very wide but on the right side of the page the handwriting becomes crowded and leaves no margin at all, the person goes through constant conflict between his generosity and his thrift. He starts out by paying a big sum of money on one fine thing or spending socially with a grand gesture, and then he tries to make up for it by a contradictory excursion into thrift.

However, when the reverse is seen, with the right-side margin very wide but the margin at the left extremely narrow, the writer also goes through much- conflict between the conscious frugality and the unconscious spurts of spending. In this instance he starts out with every good intention of sticking to the limits of his budget, but finds it difficult to maintain such a cautious attitude and ends up by generous spending.

Your Personality in Handwriting

Chapter 5

SPACES BETWEEN LINES
AND WORDS

In addition to the margins as signs of the generosity or frugality of
the writer, the spaces which appear between the lines of handwriting
and the words are also significant. Naturally, the more space that is
left open on the sheet of paper, the more is the purse open, and the
less space the tighter are the strings pulled closed on the purse.

A popular error made by the layman is that a large handwriting
portrays an extravagant person, whereas small formations mean
stinginess. It is true that some people who write large are generous,
but some of them are not; also some who make tiny formations are
frugal yet some people who write that way are generous. So that the
size of writing alone cannot be taken as a definite sign where attitude
toward finances is concerned, but the margins (discussed in previous
chapter) and the spaces are the determining factors.

A writing with wide open spaces and very large formations discloses
the person has extravagant tendencies and not only spends for his
own pleasure but likes to be generous toward others. But if the
handwriting has large spaces and is of small size, then the person is
generous in spirit but is not extravagant and shows more care in the
way he spends on others as well as for his own purposes.

In reverse, when a handwriting has hardly any space or no space
between lines of writing and the words, but the letter formations are
very large, there is a contradiction not easily understood by others.
The large writing shows that the person may think of himself as
the big spender and his manner is outgoing so that he gives this
impression to others; but the lack of space reveals that actually he is
frugal and is not the free spender he may appear to be at first meeting
with him.

Should the writing be small and the spaces very narrow, this combination shows that the thrift is not only for his own self but is quickly recognized by others. But it's not the small handwriting which is the key for the graphologist to determine the frugality of the writer; it is seen by the tightness of the spaces between lines and words.

If the sample of handwriting is submitted on a sheet of paper that has ruled lines horizontally across it, then it may be difficult to determine the natural spacing between the lines of handwriting. It is best, therefore, to study a specimen written on a sheet of unlined paper.

The following three illustrations are indicative of people who are not averse to spending:

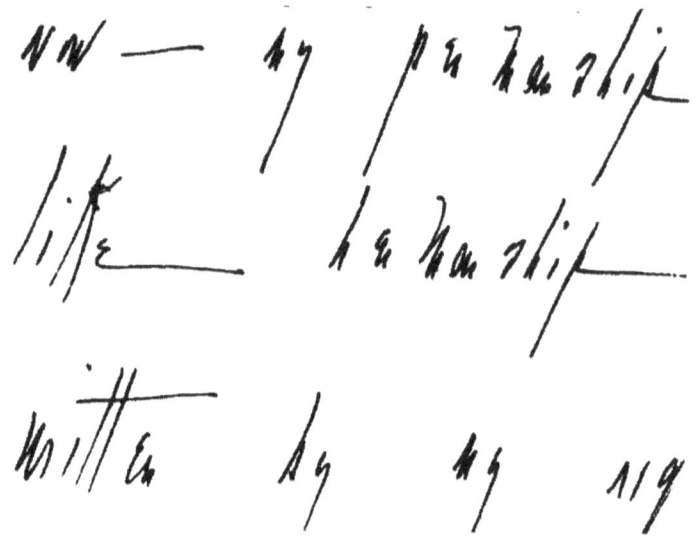

ILLUSTRATION NO. 22

This is an exaggeration of wide open spaces, but they are in keeping with style of handwriting which shows pride and a sense of grandeur. This writer desires to live on a scale befitting that attitude and the taste runs to expensive articles.

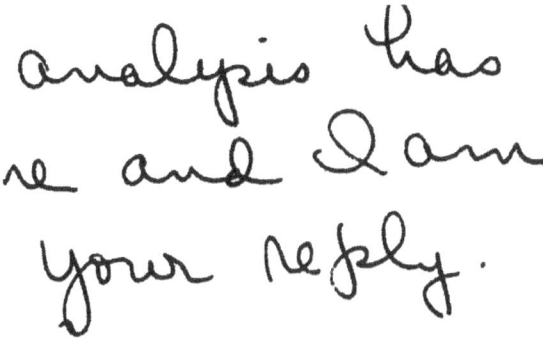

ILLUSTRATION NO. 23

These spaces are wide yet not out of proportion to the size of the letter formations. This writing shows generosity which is backed by intelligent spending for others as well as for herself.

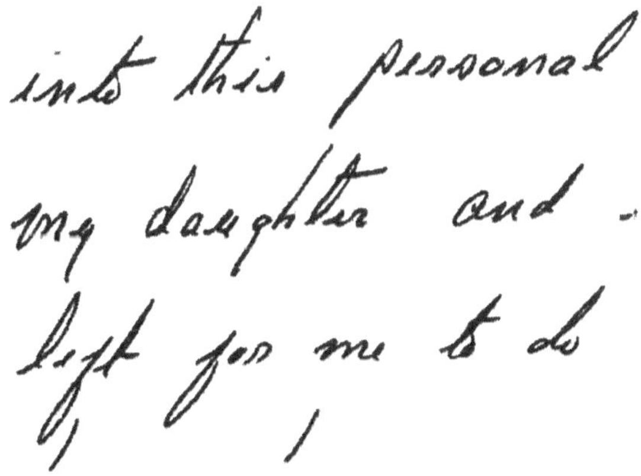

ILLUSTRATION NO. 24

This writing also has wide spaces, and they are the signs of generosity of spirit but not extravagance as the formations of the individual letters are restrained.

The following two specimens are shown for their lack of adequate spacing between words and lines of handwriting:

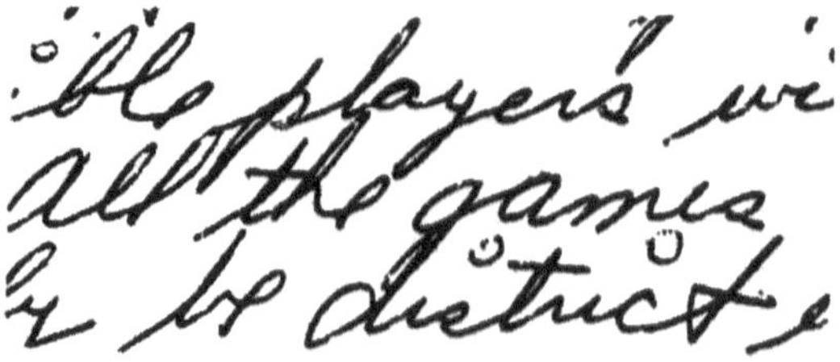

ILLUSTRATION NO. 25

Noticeable here is the way in which the bottom loop of the letters "p" and "g" reach down into the next line of writing, and the spacing between the words is also frugal. When a writer crowds the lines of handwriting together the tendency to save is much greater than the desire to spend.

ILLUSTRATION NO. 26

Here, too, the spaces between the lines of writing are too small and they run into each other. This shows all signs of the critical and cautious spender who gets full money's worth for each coin that he hands out.

The reason for giving different samples of the spenders and the savers is to show that there is not one special "type" of person in either category, and that generosity and thrift are basic traits found in all sorts of individuals.

The amount of money a person possesses does not make him generous or stingy; someone may have one dollar in his pocket and have a naturally generous spirit, whereas another may be a millionaire but still be penurious and show no generosity to others nor perhaps to his own self. In making an analysis the graphologist does not state definitely that the person does or does not spend or save, as it is impossible to know how much money the individual has or what special situations prevail merely by studying his writing. The handwriting analyst will say, "A generous spirit is shown in your writing . . ." or "You prefer to spend with caution as you are basically a thrifty person..."

Generosity is not confined to spending cash; there is generosity of spirit where the person is sincerely desirous of being of service to others even if there is no monetary transaction involved. Nor is thrift applicable only to money matters; the writing may show restraint in giving of one's self in being of service to other people. Therefore, the professional graphologist considers the motives which prompt the person in giving or withholding of himself and his services as well as his money.

Your Personality in Handwriting

Chapter 6

THE BASE LINE

In order to study the horizontal base line of the handwriting it is best to see writing done on a sheet of paper which has no ruled lines across it. When a person has to write on ruled lines there is a tendency for the handwriting to look forced and it certainly is not the natural way in which the base line would normally appear.

The mood of the writer is shown in the way the handwriting runs uphill or downhill on the sheet, or if it is written with an even base line across the page, or sometimes it may go in all sorts of directions. The base line, therefore, is the "thermometer" which registers the writer's moods and outlook on life. It is well to look at a few samples of the same person's handwriting, done at different times, to see whether it is constant for the writing to go up, down, straight across or in various directions.

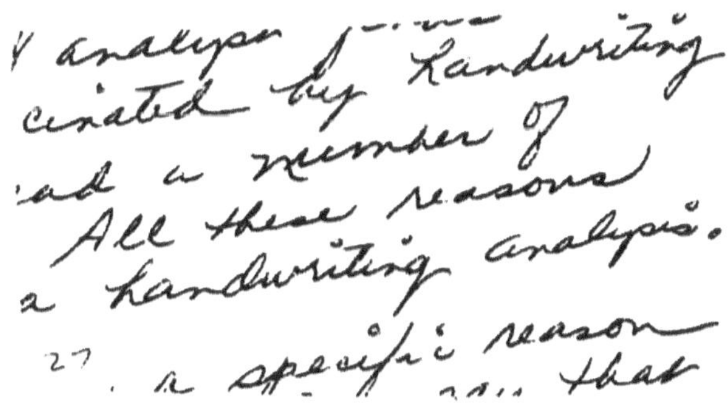

ILLUSTRATION NO. 27

This is an ascending base line; it reveals an optimistic attitude, a "looking up" toward happy times. This person does not become discouraged over each little disappointment which may occur.

31

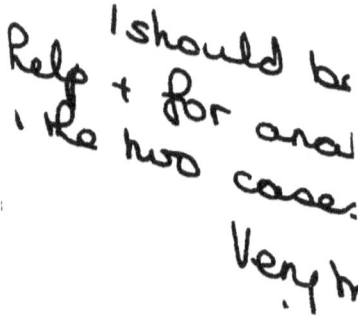

ILLUSTRATION NO. 28

The descending base line is the reverse of the foregoing specimen; here the writer has a pessimistic attitude and hesitates to proceed with any new idea unless the skeptical mind is assured that each detail is all right.

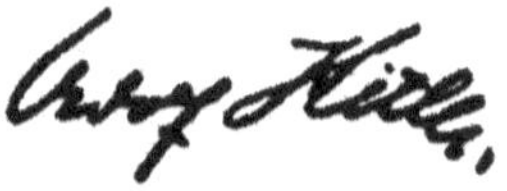

ILLUSTRATION NO. 29

When there is a sudden drop at the end of the line of writing, as seen in this specimen of Hitler's signature, it reveals the person who is greatly inhibited, unhappy because of temperamental depression, and difficult to understand. Such people generally bring misery to themselves as well as others, and that he ended up a suicide is no surprise to graphologists!

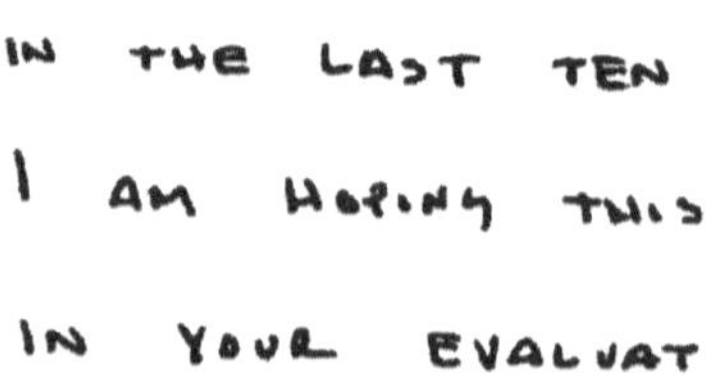

ILLUSTRATION NO. 30

The base line which is done in an even manner reveals that the writer is able to keep on an even keel without permitting the moods to get out of hand either too optimistically or too pessimistically. Of course there may be variations to this, dependent on the other signs such as size and pressure of formations (which will be shown in later chapters); but in a general sense the even base line is the sign of the person who is able to keep the moods from getting out of hand.

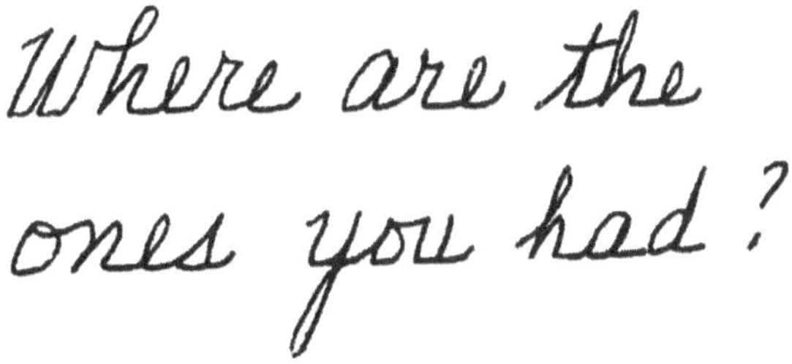

Where are the ones you had ?

ILLUSTRATION NO. 31

The unnatural or "forced" even base line, sometimes achieved by the writer using a guide-line or by slowly writing without such a guide, discloses the person who consciously controls the moods. This is usually a person of much reserve who does not permit himself to become involved or interested in things outside of his own subjective way of thinking and acting.

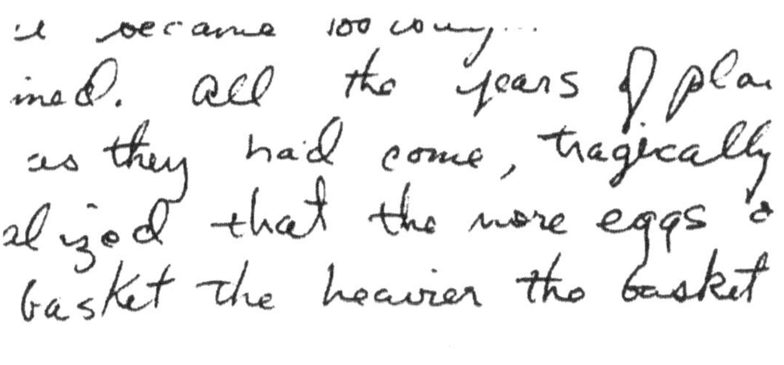

I became too confined. All the years of play as they had come, tragically realized that the more eggs a basket the heavier the basket

ILLUSTRATION NO. 32

33

The irregular base line, sometimes looking like the waves of the ocean, shows the person who has variable moods; sometimes optimistic, other times the reverse. The attitude usually depends on the situation at the moment, and the changeable moods produce a personality that is hard to know but usually very interesting to others * These people are generally full of new ideas and they don't like to be engaged in routine activities which mean attention to too many details. They are easily bored and so they need a variety of activities.

ILLUSTRATION NO. 33

In keeping with the foregoing here is Mussolini's signa¬ture which has a variable base line. This shows he had a need for many activities; but in his case there is much originality in the letter forms and he was able to control the fluctuating moods when he wanted to follow through on some definite purpose.

As in all other indications in handwriting, no one sign means one absolute thing unless it is co-related to hundreds of other signs. Therefore, whether the writing ascends or descends, or is on an even line or fluctuates, is not the final way to determine the personality; but the base line is a good starting-point for many other indications. For instance, if the base line is exaggeratedly uphill it shows an optimism and buoyancy that is out of proportion, and as a result the person may show poor judgment in appraising people and places and ideas.

If the downhill base line descends too far, that too is an exaggeration; it reveals a person who is too sensitive, too easily depressed, and his judgment is certainly not good as it is subjectively based on his own overly pessimistic attitude.

Of course these may be temporary moods of overblown optimism or heavy-laden pessimism caused by sudden situations, and those signs in the handwriting may disappear or become less exaggerated as the causative situation is cleared up. The same may be said of the uneven base line, which may become so only because of a sudden or temporary situation, and then the irregularities disappear and the even base line may again be used when the disturbing cause is cleared up. It is for this reason I suggested, in the second paragraph of this chapter, that it is best to get a few specimens of the person's handwriting done at different times, and not to rely on the sample of writing done just for the immediate purpose of a graphological analysis.

It is interesting to see the handwriting of each member in a family, or each person in a group of co-workers, or each individual who is part of a social circle, to determine which persons write with the optimistic ascending base line and those whose writing may be pessimistically descending, and the people who make even or irregular base lines. This gives a clue to the way in which they respond to one another, as well as to the outside influences in their individual lives. If, in a family or other group, some are natural optimists and others are pessimists, and some maintain a constant even attitude while others always fluctuate in mood, there might be some misunderstandings among them because of their different individual reactions to situations. When the handwritings are submitted for analyses, the graphologist is able to perform a good service to all of them by pointing out their differences as well as their similarities and so give them a good starting point toward congeniality.

Your Personality in Handwriting

Chapter 7

SLANTS OF WRITING

The graphologist finds the study of the slants very interesting — whether the writing leans forward to the right, or is done in backhand manner, or is vertical, or perhaps goes in all directions — because the slant tells whether the person is inclined to listen to the dictates of the heart or the head, or perhaps strikes a good balance or suffers a conflict between the two.

The most usual way of writing is with a slant to the right.

ILLUSTRATION NO. 34

This was written by a woman in her seventies who has retained the graciousness of manner of the mid-Victorian period. The forward-leaning slant shows a warm and affectionate heart, and she is happiest when sharing her life with others rather than being alone. Of course others who write with this same right-hand slant, but not in the same style of penmanship, will have different and individual personality traits of their own, but basically the slant shows that the heart is warm regardless of what other traits are seen in the co-relation of the other signs in the handwriting.

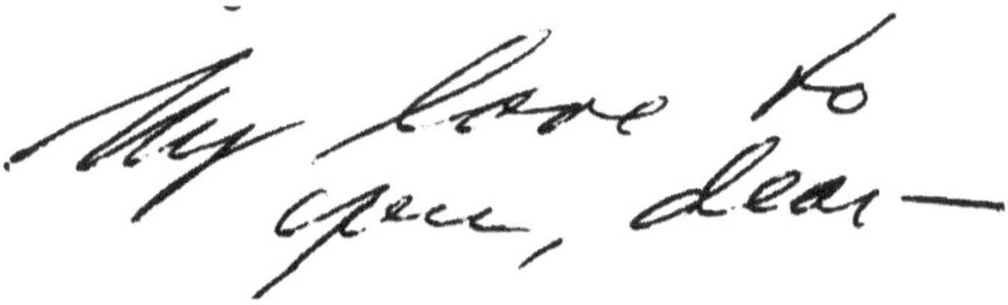

ILLUSTRATION NO. 35

The slant is more forward-leaning here, and this was written by a man in his mid-forties. You will notice this is a more extreme right-hand slant, and the sharper the to-the-right angle of writing the more ardent is the nature. People who make this slant of writing like to work where they can meet other people; the human element is always more important to them than the mechanical or clerical details of the work itself. They like to socialize and not be alone too much of the time.

Many people who were taught the forward-leaning angle of writing shift to the backhand method; this usually occurs in the teen-age period and is often done unconsciously. Of course every backhand writer does not have all traits in common, as each one has his or her own individual personality, and this is seen in the various signs of the handwriting; however, backhand writing in itself is a sign of the repression of the feelings, a hesitancy to permit the heart to take the lead. Here are some illustrations of backhand:

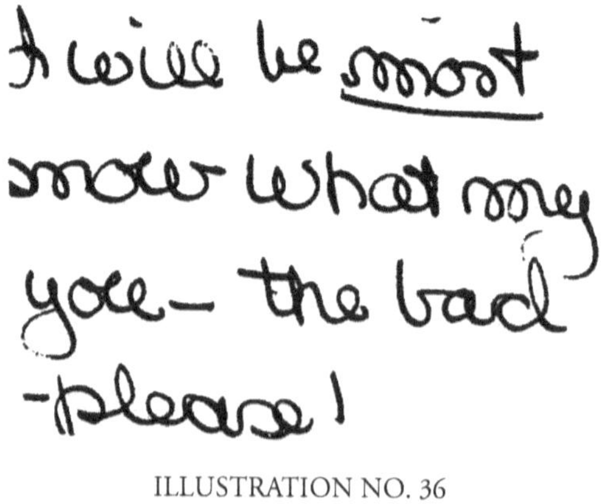

ILLUSTRATION NO. 36

This woman, in her late twenties, wrote me that her teacher insisted on the to-the-right slant, but as soon as she got out of grammar school she started to write backhand and continues to do so because it is easier for her. Of course it is, because she is naturally hesitant to meet many new people, and she doesn't have the self-confidence to let her heart make decisions. Thus she "pulls back" and so her handwriting instinctively also pulls back. The rounded formations show she likes people and is sympathetic (this is explained in a later chapter), but the backhand writing betrays her hesitancy to show her warm feelings unless someone else takes the initiative.

ILLUSTRATION NO. 37

But this backhand writing shows a more self-confident person who deliberately "pulls back" because his head wants to dominate his heart, and usually it does. And his handwriting unconsciously goes backhand. This specimen was done by a young man in his late teens.

In some cases the backhand writing is not due to the self-conscious hesitancy to come forward or the deliberate repression and control of the emotions, but it may be due to the person writing with the left hand. If the specimen of handwriting is accompanied by the information that it is done by a left-handed writer, then the graphologist must exercise great care in studying it and sometimes has to disregard the angle of the writing and concentrate on all the other personality signs.

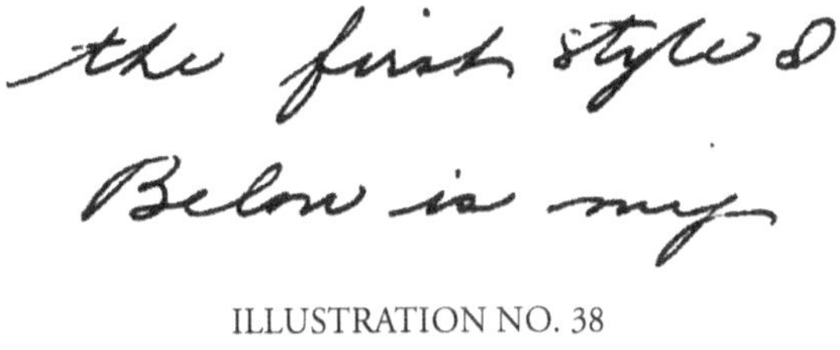

ILLUSTRATION NO. 38

39

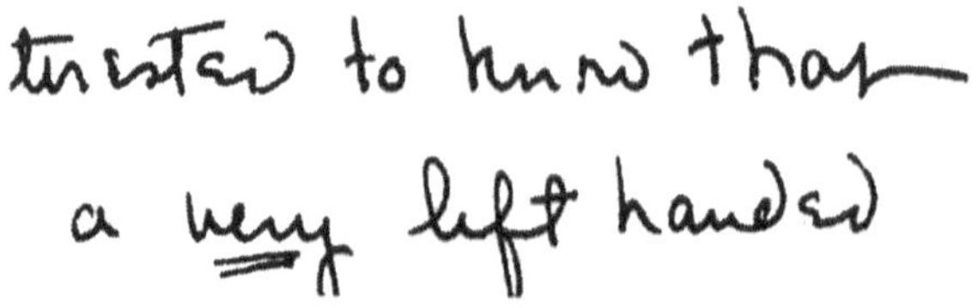

twisted to know that
a very left handed

ILLUSTRATION NO. 39

An interesting example is seen in the two styles of writing done by one women who is left-handed. She learned to write in the forward-leaning slant, and still writes that way unconsciously because it is the instinctive expression of the warmth of her affectionate heart. But when she wants to produce an effect of cool-headedness and to impress other people that she is "hard to get" she consciously writes with the backhand formations. However, the professional graphologist is able to discern the similar basic traits in both styles of her writing. When someone writes various styles with equal ease, as is the case in this specimen, there is a good deal of self-assurance in the personality make-up. This person can be most tactful in "playing a role" to suit the occasion and is able to be a diplomat when the situation demands it.

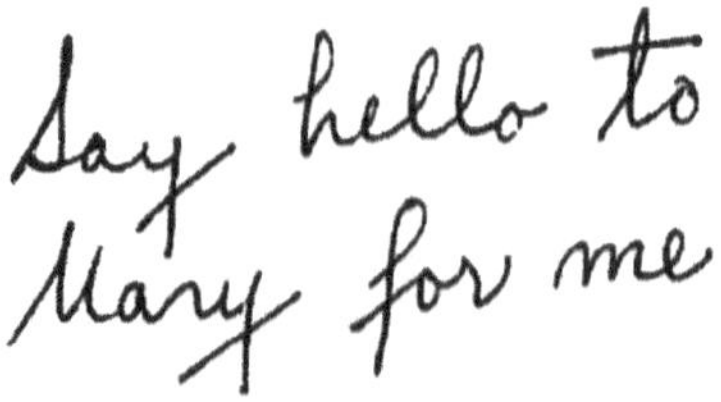

Say hello to
Mary for me

ILLUSTRATION NO. 40

When the writing is vertical the graphologist usually finds the person to have a sound balance between the heart and the head. As a rule the one who writes with vertical formations has a reserved manner and does not betray emotions on the surface. This person is disinclined to take chances and prefers to work out all ideas in a careful manner before coming to a definite decision. Generally the person who writes with vertical formations is consistent in mood and manner.

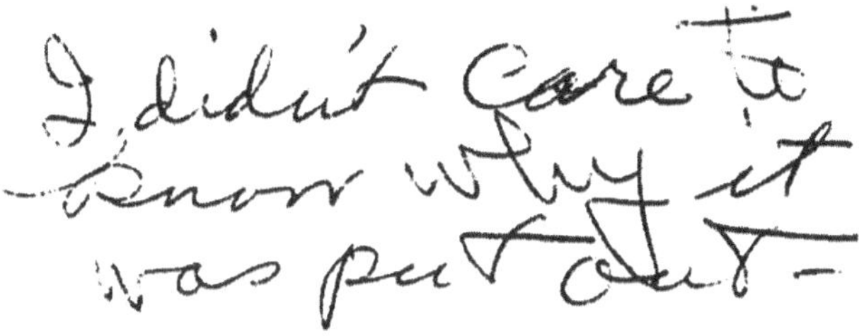

ILLUSTRATION NO. 41

When the angle of writing goes in every direction it is a sign of undisciplined emotions. These people usually "blow hot and cold" over new ideas and people and places; it is hard for them to be consistent in attitude or in action. The personalities are generally interesting because they are puzzling; one may meet this person one day and find him friendly and cooperative, the next day he may be the complete opposite. Some days he may work very hard and at other times not be able to produce a thing. These writers are usually versatile in tastes and abilities, and they go through much inner conflict between mind and emotions. It was thought at first that this variability of the angles of writing was part of the growing-up process of youth; but the graphologist finds this condition in the handwritings of adults as well. In fact, the foregoing specimen was written by a man in his late thirties.

An interesting comparative study in graphology is to get samples of writing of various people comprising a group, either a family or a committee or at a place of work, and see how many write with a right-leaning slant, how many write backhand or vertical, or go in all sorts of directions. If you find that each person in a group writes with a different angle or slant you will then have a clue as to why some of the individuals are outgoing, some restrained, some inconsistent in mood — and by pointing these things out to them you are able to establish a sounder basis for each one to recognize the fundamental traits in the others.

Chapter 8

PRESSURE

In the pressure which the writer exerts when he uses a pen or pencil he tells how he reacts to people and situations, either sensitively or aggressively. Sometimes a person who writes normally with a light pressure may show a heavier pressure when using a pen or pencil to which he is not accustomed, or the reverse may hold true. Therefore, in analyzing a handwriting and studying its pressure it is best to see a sample where the person used the pen or pencil he prefers to use, and not a writing instrument which he borrowed from someone else.

Much discussion has been occasioned since the advent of the ball-point pen as to whether writing which is done with it should be used as a basis for analysis, for the reason that variations of pressure are not discernible by the use of this newly-designed style of pen. Therefore, if possible, get a sample of writing done with a fountain pen or the pen which has an inserted nib, or even with a pencil. Some graphologists don't prefer to see handwritings done with pencil, but in some recent experiments I have given groups of ten people the same kind of No. 2 pencil (semi-soft) and asked them to write with them, and variations of pressure showed up in the handwritings they produced. Thus, the aversion on the part of some handwriting analysts against penciled writing does not always hold true.

A graphologist is often asked, "What type of pen or pencil do you recommend for me to use?" and that is something which cannot be told. Each person is the one who determines what writing instrument is best; generally the one who writes with light pressure chooses a thin pen-point or a pencil with a hard graphite. And the one who writes with heavy pressure usually chooses a heavier stub pen or a softer pencil. Just as no can choose a pair of shoes for another to wear (not knowing how comfortable they feel on the feet) so no one can select a pen or pencil for someone else because there is no way of knowing how comfortable it feels in that person's hand.

In discussing the illustrations shown in this chapter, attention is called to the fact that in reproducing them the pressures may not be shown as clearly as they are in the actual handwriting. And when a graphologist is given a photostat copy or a photograph of a specimen of writing, this same allowance is made for any deviation from the clarity in the original handwriting sample.

The pressure in handwriting is not necessarily indicative of the mental qualities of the writer; the purpose in studying it is to see the way in which the person responds to people and to environment. It is also an indication of whether the writer is inclined toward introversion or is extroverted or perhaps an ambivert.

There are varying degrees of pressure used by people in writing, but for easier understanding we will separate them into three general types — light, medium and heavy pressure — and will discuss them in that order.

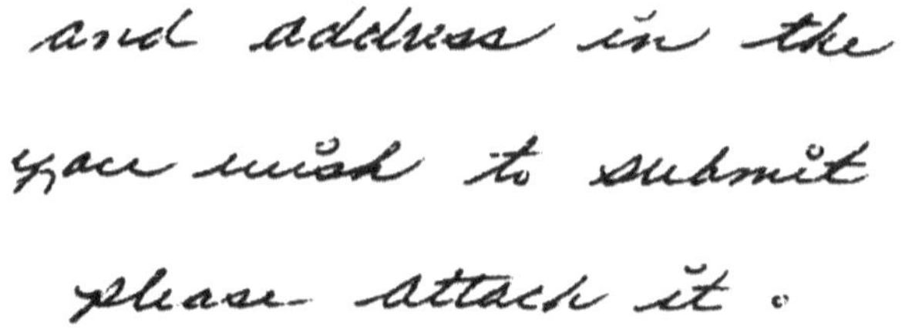

ILLUSTRATION NO. 42

Not all people who write with a light pressure have completely similar traits, as much depends on the other signs in the handwriting. But light pressure in itself is a sign of a person who is idealistic in attitude, has a tendency to introspection, and maintains a reserve about disclosing the innermost feelings except when he is very sure of the one in whom he confides. Such writers are usually sensitive in their reactions to new surroundings and to all people they meet. While some people who write lightly may undertake tasks which require leadership and prove successful (if they have other qualifying traits) they sometimes hesitate to take aggressive steps on their own. The light-pressure writer looks upon all human relationships, whether social or in business, with serious loyalty.

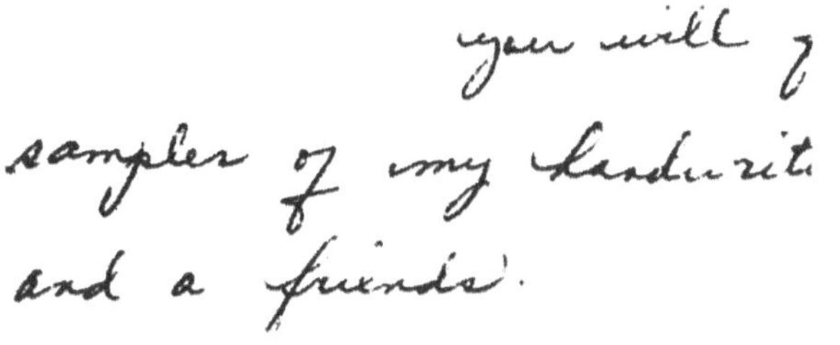

ILLUSTRATION NO. 43

The one who writes with a medium pressure of the pen or pencil is usually able to adapt with ease to each situation as it occurs; such a person is neither completely introverted nor extroverted but combines much of each and can be called the ambivert. The medium-pressure writer is not as sensitive as the one who writes lightly nor as aggressive as the one who has a heavy pressure. This person's attitude is consistent and for that reason can more easily be understood that the others.

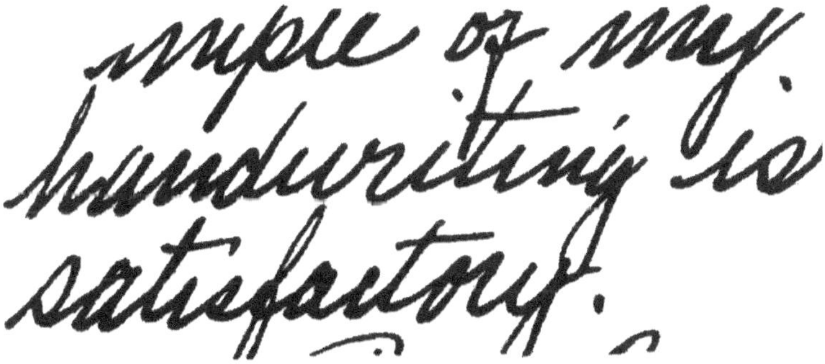

ILLUSTRATION NO. 44

Heavy pressure signifies vitality and self-assertiveness. These people like to keep active, and are usually in the category of extroverts. Even if other signs in the handwriting show idealism, these heavy-pressure writers are aware of the material needs of life. And when they love someone there is much ardor in their feelings.

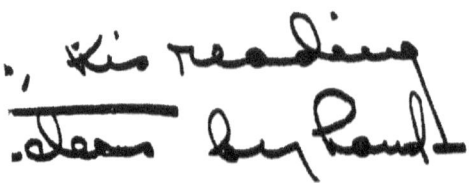

ILLUSTRATION NO. 45

In this specimen of writing the pressure is heavier on the horizontal strokes. This is a sign of much will power and a desire for good living. Such writers usually have vital personalities to which other people quickly respond, and so it is good for them to do work when they can deal with people. The heavier the pressure on the horizontal lines the more domineering is the personality, and the more desire for self-gratification.

But if the reverse holds true, when the vertical strokes are heavier than the horizontal, we have the person who secretly yearns for as much gratification as does the one who makes the heavier horizontal strokes, but is inhibited and does not have the aggressiveness to follow through. Thus while the outer manner may appear to be a defiant one (in the person who writes the vertical strokes heavier) the inner self often lacks the power to carry through.

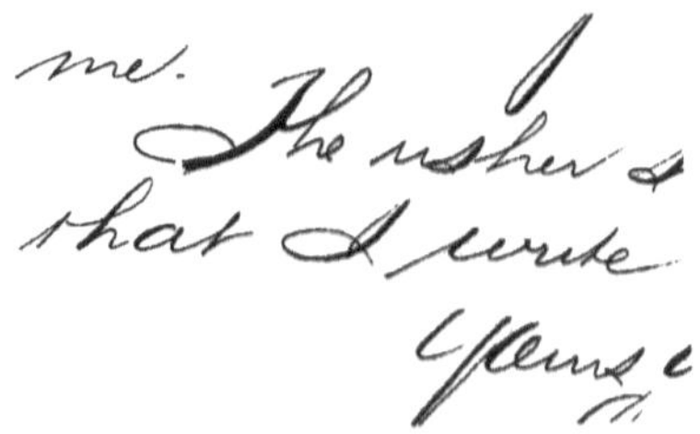

ILLUSTRATION NO. 46

This writing is not regarded as one with unconscious heavy pressure on vertical strokes as heretofore described. This style of writing is done consciously; the person deliberately produces this fancy and pictorial way of setting off his writing as a thing of beauty. It is a mark of a romantic heart, a desire for gracious living, and adherence to all the charming social niceties. This is an old-fashioned style and is indicative of a respect for tradition. The one who makes this artistic writing is persistent but is not necessarily an aggressive personality.

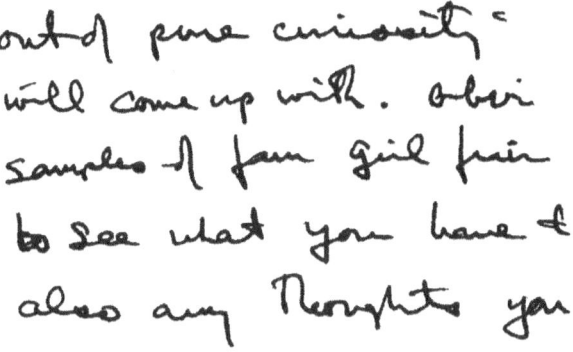

ILLUSTRATION NO. 47

When pressure is not even but varies from word to word or letter to letter, it reveals a person who has a rather fluctuating temperament, is very sensitive and not always consistent in reacting to people, surroundings, situations. Sometimes he is assertive, at other times he hesitates to go ahead. A state of indecision is shown in this sample of writing, the mind is intellectually curious, and he is alternately secretive and talkative. While some of the heavy strokes show extroversion, the rest of the signs of the writing reveal him to be much more of an introvert than appears on the surface. Another factor shown in the multi-pressure handwriting is the quickness of temper which is suddenly triggered into action and then dies out just as rapidly.

ILLUSTRATION NO. 48

Writing which is muddy-looking reveals a person who is self-indulgent, impatient, lacks refinement and sensitivity, and refuses to take part in any cooperative effort unless there is personal gain for his own self. This is a writing of physical vitality, devoid of idealism. This illustration is a copy of Napoleon Bonaparte's signature.

When a signature shows a different pressure from the rest of the writing it means that the person is putting on a facade. For instance, if the writing is of heavy pressure and the person signs lightly he is trying to impress upon the others that he is a modest fellow, whereas in reality he is aggressive. In reverse, if the writing is light in pressure and the signature is heavy, he is anxious to have people think he is self-sufficient, although the inner man is sensitive and may not be able to follow through in an aggressive manner. Therefore, when the writing and signature show contradictory pressures, the analysis must be made primarily from the handwriting itself and not from the way the name is signed.

In the examination of the handwritings of people of all ages there is no one age group which writes with a light or a medium or a heavy pressure. There is often an erroneous conception that all children write with heavy pressure and all old people write lightly. But that does not hold true, for the reason that if a child has a vital, aggressive personality the pressure of his writing will be heavier than that written by the sensitive and introverted child. And old people who are vigorous in mental attitude and physical power may write with heavy pressure, while those who are more sensitive and introspective will write with light pressure. It is not possible to place handwritings into '"types" for the reason that the way each person writes is an instinctive gesture of his or her own individual inner personality.

Chapter 9

SIZE AND WIDTH

Some people naturally write small, others write very large, and some do the in-between average size of handwriting. While the size of the writing must be studied in relationship to all other indications, of itself it is interesting to the graphologist.

The sample of writing should be studied when it is done on a sheet of paper that is not too small. For instance, when a person writes on a post card or any other small card or piece of paper, or on note-book pages which have ruled horizontal lines placed close together, he might make his formations proportionately small to fit the limited space available, whereas normally he might be a natural large-formation writer when using a regular sheet of paper.

Another thing to watch out for is a photograph or a photostatic copy of a handwriting, as very often it may be reduced in size or made larger to fit the special purpose for which it was photographed. In that case, of course, you cannot be sure of the actual size of writing and the analysis may go a bit askew because of that.

A graphologist often hears the remark, "Oh, that person is stingy because he writes small..." or "What a generous person she is, look at her large handwriting ..." yet neither of these may be correct deductions. The size of the letter formations must be studied together with the margins and the spacing which are the determining factors in such cases rather than whether the handwriting is small or large.

As a general rule small formations in handwriting reveal the ability of the mind to concentrate on details, to do work which calls for meticulous results. These people don't rush about to try out all new ideas or attend to too many jobs all at one time; they use care in thought and action. Here are two specimens of small writing:

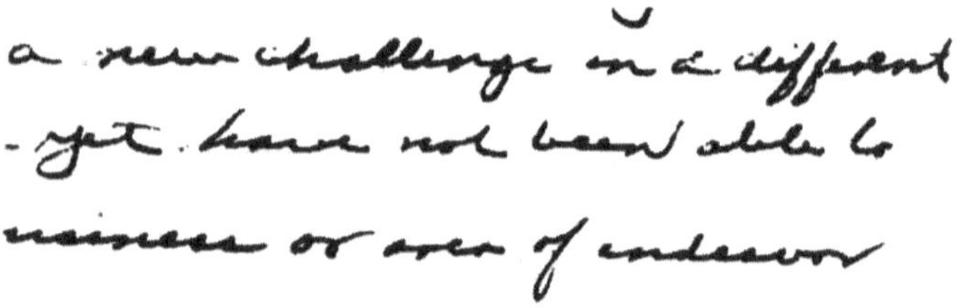

ILLUSTRATION NO. 49

This was done by a man almost sixty years of age, who has spent his entire working life and is still actively engaged in the field of accountancy. The words do not have large spaces between them, which shows that he is a careful person even in his personal life aside from his work. He does not take chances, but prefers to work out each idea in careful detail.

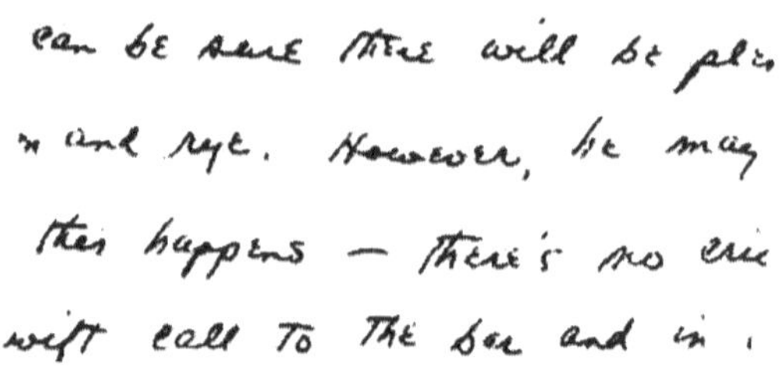

ILLUSTRATION NO. 50

A woman of about forty, who is an editor, wrote this sample of small handwriting. Here you will see that her spaces between the words are wide, which shows her interest in people and her generosity of spirit; but her mind is capable of critical thought. She applies herself to her editorial work with concentration and efficiency.

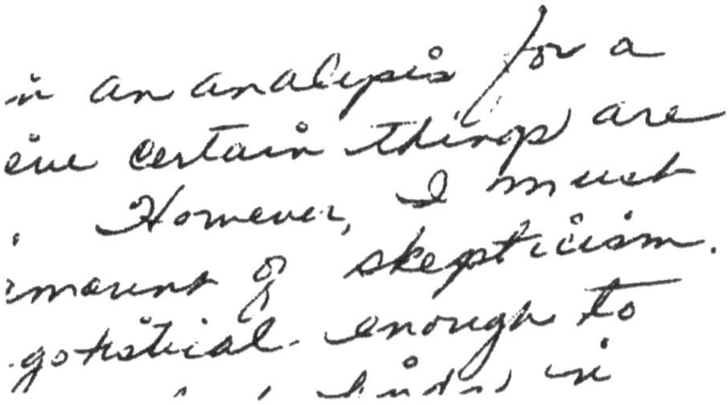

ILLUSTRATION NO. 51

Writing which is neither small nor large, but just a happy medium, shows the person who has just that kind of attitude toward life. The mind and heart usually work together. There is an interest in what is going on, yet the ability to hold back when necessary and not too outgoing in personality. This illustration is from a woman of thirty who is married, a home-maker who also does much work in charity organizations.

A person who writes with medium size formations is usually not difficult to understand as she (or he) is more ready to get along with all sorts of people; that is, with the careful thinkers like the ones who write small and with the more gregarious people who write large.

We now come to the large handwritings, and the following three illustrations show variations even though all are done with big formations:

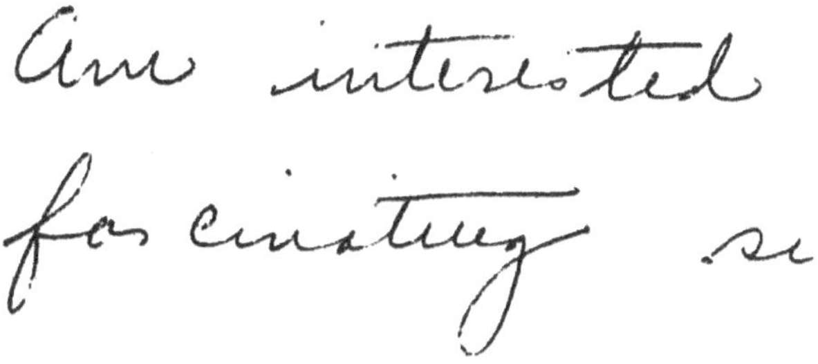

ILLUSTRATION NO. 52

Here the spaces between the words and the lines of writing are large, showing that she is outgoing and has a friendly personality, that she would certainly not care for work where she would have to be in a routine of details all the time. Nor would she be happy in a social life that was limited to just one or two persons; she is gregarious and needs to meet many people. This was written by a woman in her late forties, a home economist who goes out to talk to clubwomen on food and entertaining, a profession which is admirably suited for her.

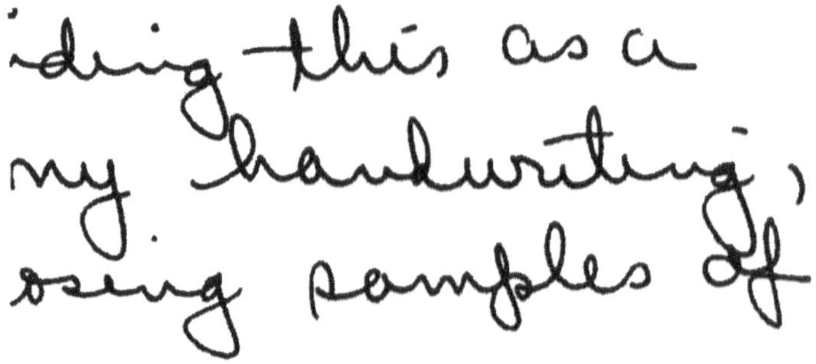

ILLUSTRATION NO. 53

This, too, is a fairly large handwriting from a woman in her early thirties who is employed as a secretary. Her job affords her the opportunity to meet many people and to participate in a variety of chores in connection with her work. She is, therefore, well-suited to her job, she could not be happy in one which would be confining in routine details or would not give her a chance to meet new people. Even though this specimen shows a tendency to backhand slant of writing it is also large and wide, and thus counteracts the reserve which is usually found in a writing which is done in backhand style. This, then, is an instance where the exception and not the rule has to be taken into consideration; and it is pointed out to show that not one sign can mean the same in every individual specimen of handwriting.

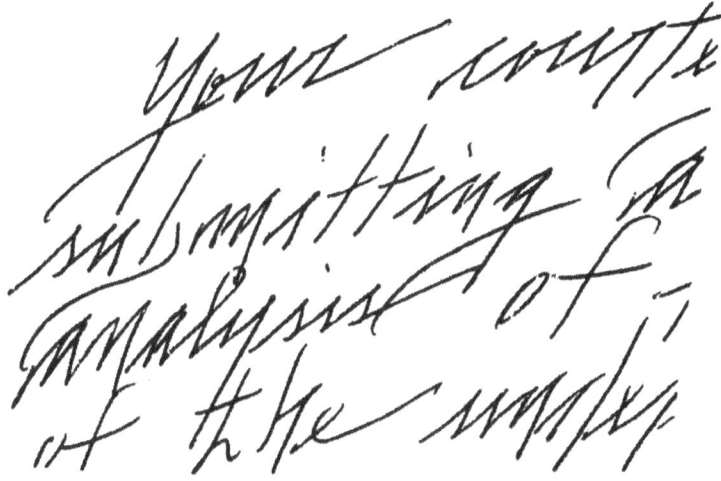

ILLUSTRATION NO. 54

We come now to another exception to the general rule of the large handwriting which normally indicates a gregarious interest. In this man's writing we find the letters are written with angular formations and there is often an inner conflict between his desire to try out many new ideas and meet many sorts of people, and his other more critical self which keeps pulling him back into himself and doesn't accept too freely the ideas of other people. This person is willing to try new ideas of his own, and in his work as a tool designer he evidently finds full scope for this desire.

It may seem confusing to the student of graphology to try and understand these exceptions by studying all separate phases of the handwriting and then putting them together through the process of adding and subtracting, and arriving at the result in that way rather than in relying just on what one sign shows. Much patience and study are required, and especially so when it comes to the size of the writing and its relationship to the other indications.

You may come across a handwriting where there are variations in the size of the writing; on one sheet you may find small and medium and large formations all used by the same person. If the writing is basically a small one and occasionally some larger formations are injected, the variation in size may mean the person is very sensitive and may find it difficult to concentrate too long on one subject even though he is capable of doing so when he is in calmer mood and not suffering any hurt feelings. But when the normally large handwriting shows some smaller formations, the person is perhaps going through some inner emotional conflict which is not seen on the surface. Of course, no hasty conclusion can be reached in a general sense, and each handwriting must be studied individually when there are variations of size; but in any case the writer is not too easy to understand and may be undergoing some very sensitive and emotional feelings which he is trying to keep to himself.

There is often in a handwriting a disproportion between the size of the capital letters and the small letters. When the capitals are neither too large nor too small they don't need to be studied separately for an analysis; that is, where the matter of size is concerned.

But if you find large capital letters in a very small handwriting they disclose a good deal of pride as well as self-confidence, even though the small writing indicates the mind that concentrates on details. Such people are usually quite surprising to others, who are puzzled about reconciling the proud self-confidence and the ability of the writer to be alone and think through all ideas in a careful manner.

When the reverse is seen, where the capital letters are much smaller than the rest of the handwriting, the graphologist knows that the personality is not as self-confident or proud as the writer might desire to be. The one who makes small capital letters in a writing too large in proportion is not sufficiently self-assertive.

The width of the writing is regarded as the size and space of the letters from side to side (rather than their actual size up-and-down).

Kindly refer to specimens Nos. 52 and 53 which are written with wide spaces not only between the words, but also between the letters in the words and the handwritings are rounded. These people are naturally friendly and wouldn't relish any long periods of solitude. But examine specimen No. 54 where you will also see wide spaces between the words but here the writing is done in angular formations;

this is a further sign of his concern with his own ideas and not so much with other people.

Specimen No. 50 also shows wide spaces, but in a small writing. The spaces emphasize her interest in people even though her mind concentrates on her exacting work. But specimen No. 49 does not have wide spaces with the small handwriting, and this brings out his care in choosing his companions and his ability to maintain his reserve in human relationships.

The medium-size writing in specimen No. 51 has medium-wide spaces, although occasionally a wider space does show. However, the full page of her writing (not shown here) was done with medium-size spaces in proportion to the size of the handwriting. This bears out the fact that her approach to people and to work is a well-balanced one, neither too assertive nor too shy.

A general rule, then, is that the wider the spaces between words and between individual letters in the words the more outgoing is the personality, and the narrower the spaces the more reserved.

Chapter 10

ROUNDED AND ANGULAR LETTERS

When a child learns to write the letters are made in rounded form, especially in the joined-together cursive handwriting. In more recent years some schools teach the first-graders to write in manuscript style (block printing) and even in that style the disconnected letters take on a rounded form rather than being angular.

As the person matures the handwriting may become angular in places where there were previously curves in the formations. Although there are many variations in the ways of forming the letters, the four general classifications are shown in this illustration:

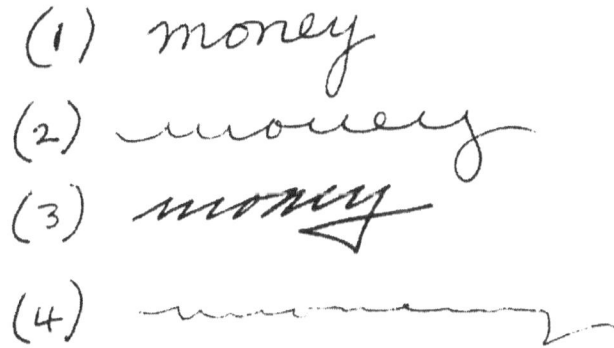

ILLUSTRATION NO. 54 A

The first one with the rounded formations is called "arcade" writing; the second one is the "garland" form, and here the curves are under the letter and not on top where they belong; the third example is the "angular" with points appearing where there should be curves; the fourth one is the "threadlike" writing which is almost formless.

The rounded "arcade" handwriting is usually indicative of the person who is not self-assertive but who prefers to work with and for other people. This person wants to get along with others, whether it be in social or business matters, or in school if the writer is still young and a student. As a rule it is much easier to understand the person who writes with rounded formations than the one who writes angularly. Of course the size and pressure of the writing and all the other signs should be taken into consideration, aside from the shape of the letter, and here are three different illustrations of rounded writing:

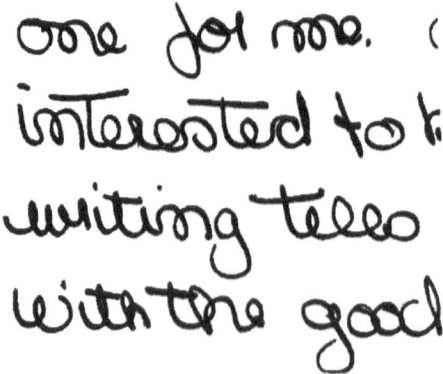

ILLUSTRATION NO. 55

This is the small and light-pressure handwriting of a young person who is mild, not a bit aggressive, who prefers to have someone else take the initiative and then he goes along in a spirit of cooperation. This is the writing of a gentle person who would never deliberately want to hurt anyone or to be at odds with anybody. All the signs of a conformist are seen here.

ILLUSTRATION NO. 56

But in this illustration the "arcade" formations are done with heavy pressure and are fairly large in size, so they reveal a person who has a desire for independent expression but does not really assert herself. This writer is not as gullible and gentle as the rounded handwriting No. 55, but is still not aggressive and the "arcades" shows that.

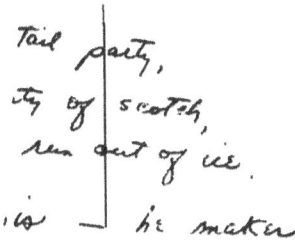

ILLUSTRATION NO. 57

When the rounded writing is very small and clearly legible it is a sign of a rare combination of a personality that is not aggressive plus a mind that is keen and searching. The heart is sympathetic and cooperative, but the mind is careful and individualistic.

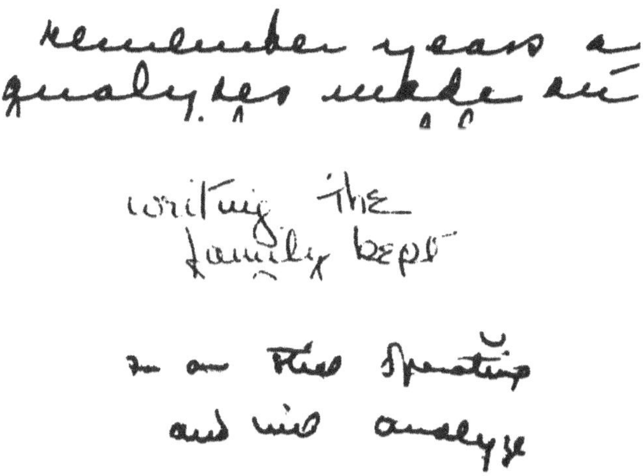

ILLUSTRATION NO. 58

59

These three samples show the "garland" formations where the letters "m" and Y are made the same way as the V and Y. This is the sign of the person who wants to be in finest surroundings and meet interesting people, who likes to dress well and live on a high scale. In looking for work this writer wants a job where the surroundings and people are stimulating and where there is a social side to the work in addition to the usual details of the job. The one who writes with "garlands" acts, as a general rule, in a tactful manner with a conscious desire to create a favorable impression on others.

When the writing is done with angular formations, the person is more critical and less gullible than the one whose writing is rounded. Of course here, too, one must consider the other factors such as size, pressure, slant, and various other signs in the writing. However, angular formations by themselves show a person who is concerned with facts, who will work hard in order to produce results of his own without needing to conform to all that other people do and say. There is usually self-assertiveness in angular writing, and if the person writes with large and heavy formations this may be seen in his outer manner; but if the angular writing is small and light in pressure the manner may seem very quiet but the mind is able to work out ideas critically and carefully. Generally the angular writer is not easily influenced by others, is not willing to make compromises on anything that is not of personal interest. The following illustrations show three different angular handwritings:

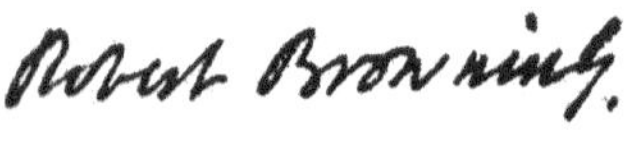

ILLUSTRATION NO. 59

The contrast in the signatures of Robert Browning, the poet, and Alfred Smith, the politician, is interesting. While both are done with angular formations, the poet's small and light-pressure writing shows his intellectual courage while the politician's heavy pressure and large formations reveal his physical as well as mental courage and assertiveness.

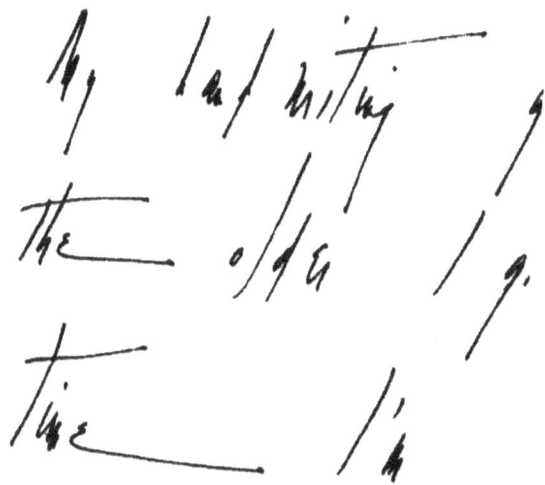

ILLUSTRATION NO. 60

This angular writing is highly stylized and is not as clear to the reader as the two angular signatures shown as examples of this type of letter formation. There is something very dramatic in this writing; it shows a person who is individualistic in thought and who desires to follow a path of work and social life where there is independence and not conformity. Yet, this writing is so consciously stylized that the angularity is not as instinctive as in the other specimens, and in many ways this writer is sensitive and is anxious for approbation from others. The angularity of the writing shows a conscious restraint of emotions, and not an unconscious gesture of self-confidence as in the two signatures shown where the angular formations are done without deliberate thought.

Generally speaking, the person whose handwriting is rounded will usually show his feelings more obviously to others and is more dependent on association with other people than the one who writes with angular formations. The latter is able to think and work independently of others, and is able to keep his feelings to himself if he thinks it is best not to disclose them. But that doesn't mean that the angular writer is incapable of cooperation or deep affection. Actually this person may be most helpful in working with and for others, and may have a most romantic heart; but is not as demonstrative in display of such feelings as the one who writes in a rounded manner.

Some people write both rounded and angular and these formations must be studied in their proper relationship to each other. When a handwriting consists mainly of rounded letters and occasionally some angles appear in it, this signifies that the writer is cooperative in spirit but also possesses some critical faculty of mind which may tone down some of the gullibility.

When a rounded handwriting includes angular capital letters the analysis must be made of the writing itself and not the capitals. The angular form of the capital letter is indicative of the desire to create an impression of being hard to know, yet the rounded small formations show the person is not truly aggressive but is easy to get along with in a cooperative sense.

But if in an angular writing you see rounded capital letters, it is a sign of a shrewd person whose outer personality seems most friendly and cooperative. However, this writer is just putting on this charming manner as a facade, whereas he is critical and self-confident and sometimes a difficult person to know.

We now come to the "threadlike" writing which in some cases is more legible than others, as shown in these two examples:

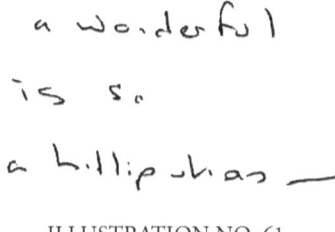

ILLUSTRATION NO. 61

The first sample of writing is fairly legible in its printed form, although the pen hardly touches the page on which it is written and just flows along. But sample No. 62 is illegible, and the threadlike writing is merely motion rather than having any actual form. To stipulate any one reason which prompts the writer to make these threadlike strokes is impossible; all other signs in the handwriting must be studied most carefully to determine if the cause is due to impatience or haste, or to inner conflicts between mind and emotions, or to utter disregard of convention, or to indecision, evasiveness, intuition, a desire to escape from any unpleasant situations, or perhaps to intellectual creativeness and versatility. Whatever the cause for this threadlike writing, it is certainly a sign of a person who is not of the usual mold as far as conformity of thought or action is concerned.

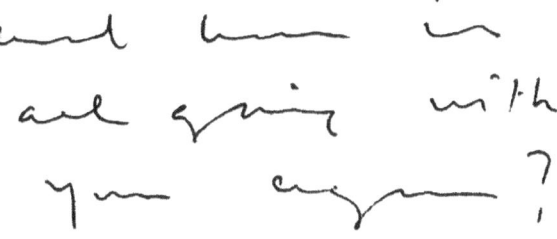

ILLUSTRATION NO. 62

Chapter 11

WORD FORMATIONS

Aside from the meanings of the individual letter formations, the way the words are made is also significant in the analysis of a handwriting. Whether the letters in each word are connected or disconnected, and if the words start out large and taper down small or are written reversely, are all interesting signs for the graphologist.

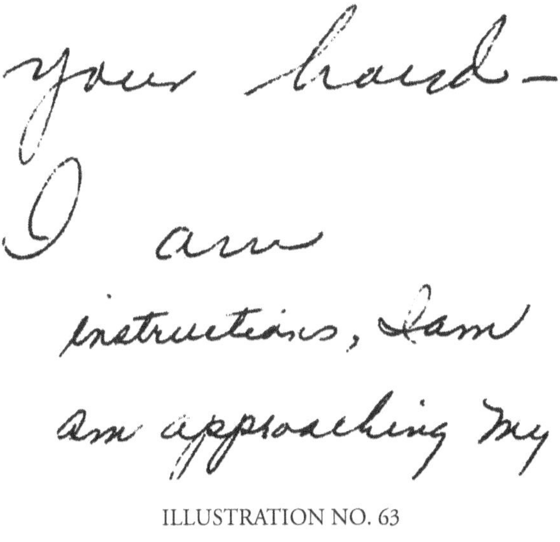

ILLUSTRATION NO. 63

When the pen or pencil does not get lifted up while the word is written, but all the letters are connected, it is a sign of a mind that likes to work things out in a careful manner. Such writers prefer not to undertake plans which seem to lack foundation. Their conclusions are usually based on logical reasoning and not on intuitive reactions. You will notice two different handwritings in the preceding illustration. Both have connected letters in each word, yet the first example shows wide spaces between the letters and the words, while the second handwriting is written with tighter spaces. So while both think in a logical manner, the writer who makes the wide spaces has a more generous and broad-minded attitude toward the ideas of others and is more willing to listen to them even if there is no immediate agreement. However, the one who writes with the narrower spaces is more cautious and will spend much time in critical appraisal of each new idea before his own mind undertakes the effort of reasoning them out to a conclusion. This, then, is an example of how one sign in a handwriting — namely, connected letters in a word — need not have a completely similar meaning in every instance, and that all other signs must be examined by the handwriting analyst.

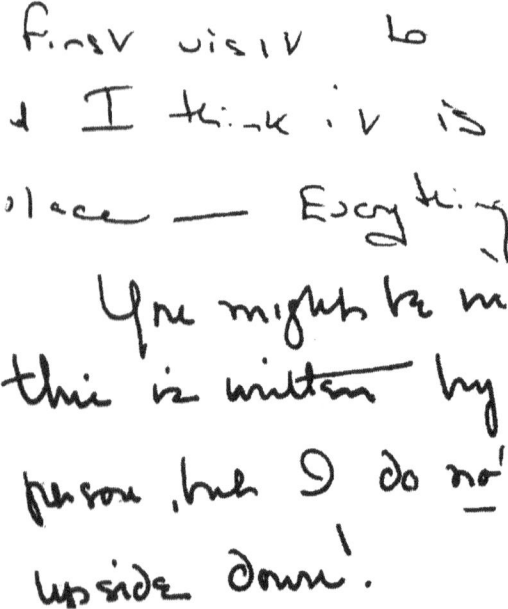

ILLUSTRATION NO. 64

When the letters in the words are completely or partially disconnected, the indication is that the writer is intuitive in response to people and places and ideas. The mind works fast, sometimes too much so, and it is sometimes irksome to these people to take time in working out each detail of a plan. They usually think and work in spurts, depending on their enthusiasm and the spontaneous reactions they have to all new situations. It is not easy for such writers to stick to jobs where they must work in routine fashion; they become restless if there are too many details which need careful attention.

Of course the intuition may be more acute in some handwritings, and less keen in others. In the illustration shown here, the first specimen is completely disconnected and in threadlike writing. This person relies entirely on intuition and would find it almost impossible to concentrate on any idea in a logical manner. But the second specimen shows partial disconnection of the letters while some of the words are fully connected, and the formations are done with clarity. While this person has many intuitive responses, the mind is capable of logical reasoning, thus producing a good balance between intuition and logic which is helpful to this writer in coming to quick and sound conclusions.

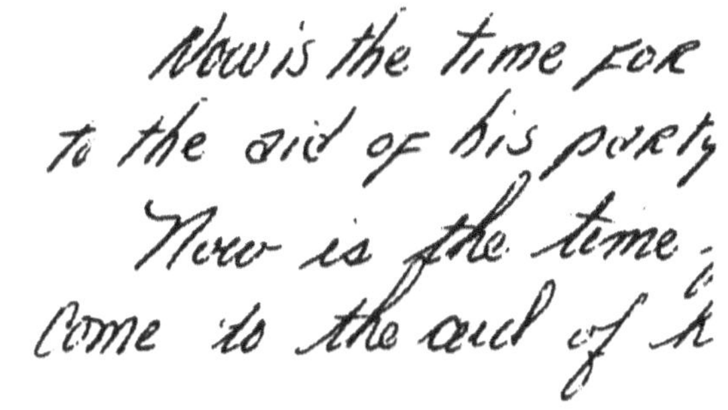

ILLUSTRATION NO. 65

This illustration is an example of printed formations which have spaces between the letters, but which must not be considered in the same way that we study the spaces in a cursive handwriting. This specimen of printed and cursive writing was done by the same person, who needs to use the printed forms for working on charts, yet who uses the cursive writing for personal letters. Therefore, the spaces which appear between the letters in a "printed" handwriting are not be regarded as a sign of intuition. If a person writes both ways it is fair to the graphologist (and to the subject of the analysis) to see samples of the two ways of writing in order to have a more complete picture of the personality that is being analyzed. In studying illustration No. 65 the analysis should be done from the cursive writing; this shows the connecting letters in the words which indicate the logical mind.

The next thing to study, in the formation of words, is whether the size of the writing changes within the word. Sometimes the word starts with a small letter and ends with a very large final letter. And there may be the reverse, where the word starts with a largely formed letter and then it tapers down so that last letter is a tiny one. Or it may start with a well-formed first letter and then slither down to a thin serpentine line at the end. Let us see the meanings of these:

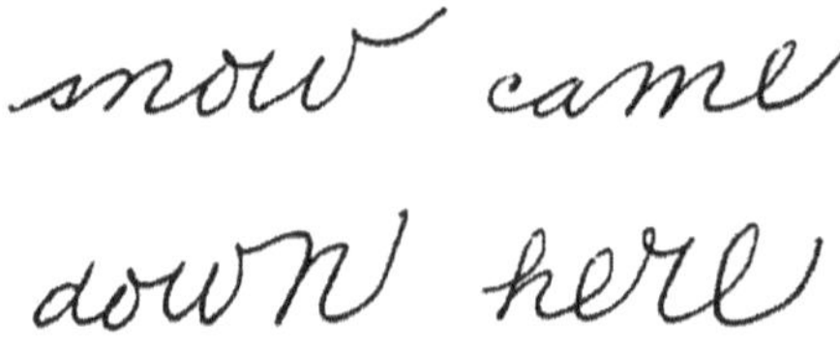

ILLUSTRATION NO. 66

This illustration shows words which start with a small letter and end up with a larger one. It is common for many children to write this way and we know it is due to their not keeping things to themselves because of lack of experience and judgment. But as they grow older most of them stop doing this and make the individual letters in the words more uniform in size. However, when an adult makes these from-smaller-to-larger letters in words, it signifies the person cannot keep a secret. Even though he may try to do so the result is that all is told and nothing is kept in confidence.

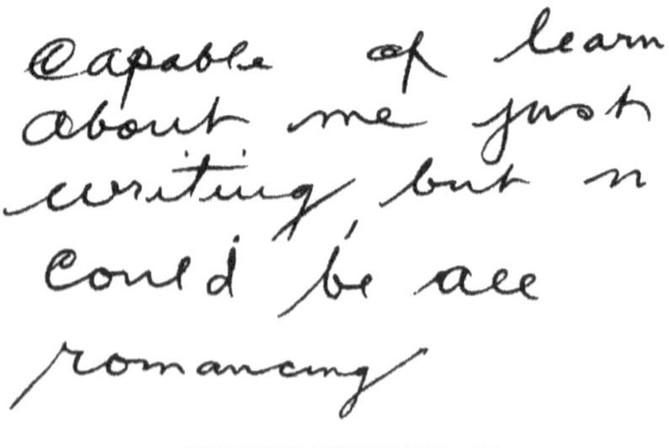

ILLUSTRATION NO. 67

Here is the reverse. You will notice in the word "romancing" the first letter is very large in proportion to the way the final letter of the word is made. You will also see this in "all" and "capable" and some of the other words, although to lesser extent. This tapering-down shows secretiveness; the person can talk most fluently and charmingly but will not divulge any more than he thinks the listener should be told.

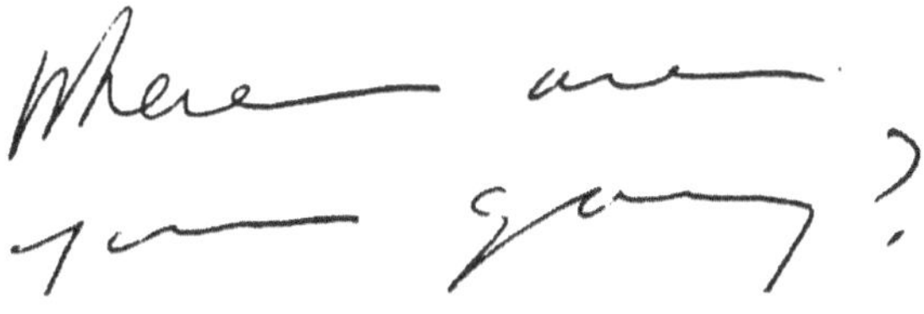

ILLUSTRATION NO. 68

When the words start out with distinguishable letter formations and then slither down into a thin line, we have an exaggeration of the secretive handwriting in specimen No. 67. There may be a variety of reasons why the person writes in this manner; primarily it denotes secrecy, and to that may be added diplomacy or evasiveness, and in some cases it shows much individuality of thought, pride, usually a high mentality. However, it is not easy for the graphologist to say this serpentine writing is definitely just one sign, and it has to be studied in conjunction with the other indications in the writing.

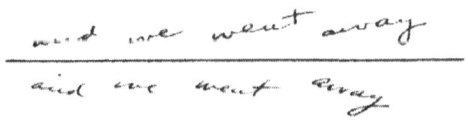

ILLUSTRATION NO. 69

Words which start at the base line and go upwards signify the person who tries to act in a cautious manner, but that is usually overcome by the optimism which is the natural state of mind. Such a writer may hesitate at first, but the enthusiasm gathers momentum as a plan proceeds. The personality is inclined to be reserved but it "warms up" very soon and the innate friendliness comes through. This writer might hesitate at first to give a promise, but usually ends up doing twice as much.

But the words which start high and descend at the final letter show the person who may start out with all enthusiastic intentions, yet the innate caution asserts itself and tones down the initial optimism. Such a person may give a promise in the first burst of enthusiasm and then regret it when he has time to reconsider.

Chapter 12

SMALL LETTERS

It is not possible to go through the twenty-six letters of the alphabet and tell what each one specifically means, for the reason that many of the letters by themselves have no significance except as they are parts of the words and sentences in which they appear.

Generally speaking, the following illustrations are given as sign-posts along the road to analysis of the handwriting:

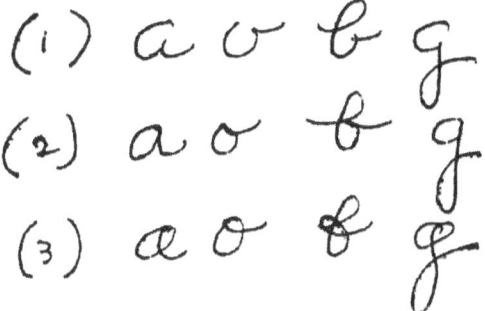

ILLUSTRATION NO. 70

Here you see the same letters written first in an open manner, then closed, and finally knotted. The first one (the open letter) is. done by the person who is usually gullible, is not able to keep quiet about things told in confidence, and betrays his own feelings.

But the second example, where the letters are closed, signifies the person is not gullible, and is able to use more judgment about what to tell or not to tell.

And the third sample, where the letters are closed by knots, shows a person who is more skeptical, who will not talk out of turn, and is able to keep his own feelings to himself.

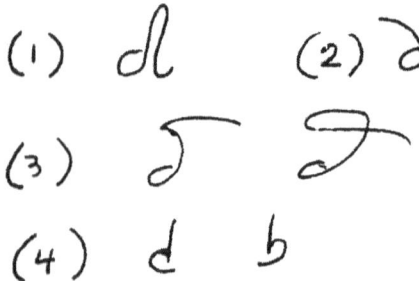

ILLUSTRATION NO. 71

The small letter "d" is often made in unusual forms. Sample No. 1 is usually known to graphologists as the "straddle d" and generally reveals a person who is considerate of other people; it is also a sign of tact or secretiveness.

Sample No. 2 is called the "Greek d" or the "cultured d" and usually shows a person who is interested in literature or music or art, or all three; but this must be studied in close relationship to other signs in the handwriting. If this "Greek d" appears in a writing which otherwise does not show any good taste or intellectual quality, then it may just be a "showing off" sign of a superficial interest in culture and is not taken seriously by the graphologist.

When this "d" turns around and the stroke comes back to the right, sometimes plain and at other times with a flamboyant curlicue at its tip, it shows an interest in culture. But stronger than that is the love of pleasure and the desire to meet people who have made intellectual and artistic strides. The interest in matters of culture is not so deep-seated as when the "d" ends in a simple, short stroke to the left.

The "d" and the "b" which turn back on themselves reveal introspection; this writer has a tendency to go back "into himself" rather than to come forward to meet other people.

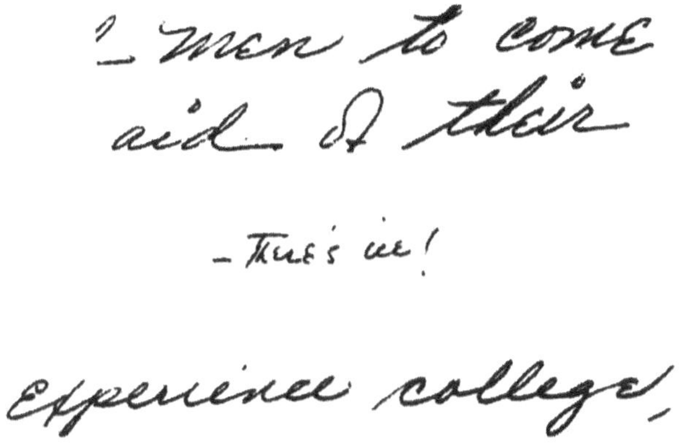

ILLUSTRATION NO. 72

The letter "e" which looks like the reverse of the figure: "3" is sometimes found in the script of a cultivated person who may also use the "Greek d" in the handwriting. But should there be no other indications of intellect and good taste in the writing, this small letter "e" by itself reveals the person to have aspirations of culture without necessarily possessing the basic elements of mind or character which could attain such a fine state of intellect andl good taste. The one who makes this "e" generally likes; to have fine things and is anxious to be in surroundings; which afford the opportunity to meet interesting and unusual people. So that even if the rest of the handwriting doesn't bear out the capacity for culture, the writer is given credit for having a desire for self-improvement.

You will see in illustration No. 72 three different handwritings in which this "e" appears. In the first and second samples the writers consistently use the "e" even though they are two distinctly different personalities. But in the last line the writer uses both the conventional V as well as the "e" we are discussing; in this case the aspiration is not as definite and consistent as with the first two writers.

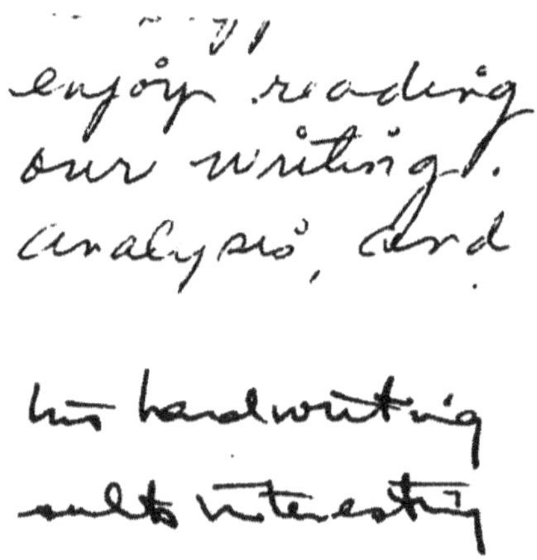

ILLUSTRATION NO. 73

The dot over the letter "i" is often not merely a dot but it takes on all sorts of shapes. For instance, see the two specimens in this illustration.

The first sample shows little circles over the "i" and her four-page letter consistently had those circles over every "i" that appeared in the writing. The significance of this unusual formation is the desire of the writer to live in surroundings of beauty, to engage in some form of activity which is related to art and in some cases to music. There is often the ability to work at some form of applied art or musical performance. This person may also like to live in an unconventional manner; but, if the rest of the handwriting points to a cautious and conservative nature, the desire to enter into any unconventional pattern of life may be only a day-dream and the writer may lack the self-assertiveness to break away from tradition.

The second specimen shows the "i" dotted with a line that is made with a blunt and heavy pressure, and two out of three of those so-called dots slant downward to the right. This shows definite viewpoints and the mind is not influenced by others; it also reveals an aggressive person who does not want to be in any subordinate position, either in work or in personal life.

74

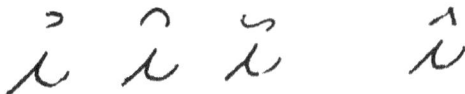

ILLUSTRATION NO. 74

Another example of "i" dots which are not dots are the funny little shapes they take. A magnifying glass, when used to examine the "i" dots, often shows many amusing formations. This applies to the letter "j" as well.

The first three "i's" in this illustration show some unusual dots, and in this example their size is purposely exaggerated to emphasize their departure from the conventional dot. These wavy shapes reveal a sense of humor.

The "i" with the tent-shaped dot over it discloses a critical mind. Whether evaluating people or things or places, such a writer has to find out "what makes it tick" and takes nothing for granted.

Now, what about the conventional "i" dot? If the dot is done with light pressure it shows more sensitivity than if made with heavy pressure; the latter is done by the person who is aggressive.

When the dot is placed very close to the letter "i" it reveals a careful mind, not given to flighty imagination. But when the dot is placed a little higher, but still directly above the letter, it also shows sound judgment but there is a more highly developed imagination. The writer may not always arrive at conclusions through practical measures.

If the "i" dots are always made the same way they reveal a person who is consistent in mind and action. But in one handwriting there may be all sorts of "i" dots; in that case the writer may have a lively imagination, is versatile or perhaps inconsistent, and doesn't prefer to live or work in a routine manner.

Occasionally a handwriting does not include any "i" dots, or only some of the letters are dotted. An "i" calls for a dot, and if the writer omits it the conclusion is that there is either lack of concentration or a poor memory where details are concerned, especially if they are not of essential interest to the writer.

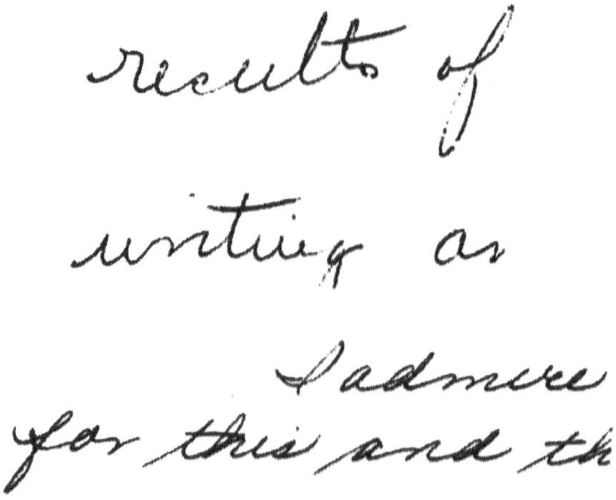

ILLUSTRATION NO. 75

The small letter "r" is often made in two ways by the same person. This is not of any real significance, and the only reason it is mentioned here is that very often the graphologist is asked by people why they make the two styles, especially as they feel that one of the formations is too old-fashioned. This is the second kind of "r" shown in both samples in illustration No. 75. Well, there is no need to think this is out-of-style because while the top sample of writing is done by a woman in her late forties the second sample is from a girl in her junior year in college. And what could be more contemporary than the young age of this writer? This so-called old-fashioned "r" is a sign of conventionality, so that even though the ideas and the work done by these people may be of modern vintage there is an underlying conventionality in the personality make-up which usually asserts itself.

The only outstanding significance found in the "r" is when it is made conspicuously larger and more squarish in appearance than the rest of the letters in a word. The overblown "r" reveals a desire for fashionable and expensive clothes; the writer wants to be well-dressed, is attracted to people of good appearance and likes to be in interesting and luxurious surroundings. Many people (especially females) who are engaged in the fashion field write with the large wide "r" and it is also found in the handwriting of some interior decorators. These writers can usually develop a gracious maner in dealing with the public, even if they are not instinctively that way.

The small letter "s" is often made like a printed form, even in cursive handwriting. Sometimes two different forms of the V are used by one writer, as shown in the two samples in illustration No. 76. This shows, generally, a person of versatility. Of course it may indicate other things; when taken into consideration with the other signs in the handwriting; for instance, it may be inconsistency, or dislike for routine and details, or great originality which

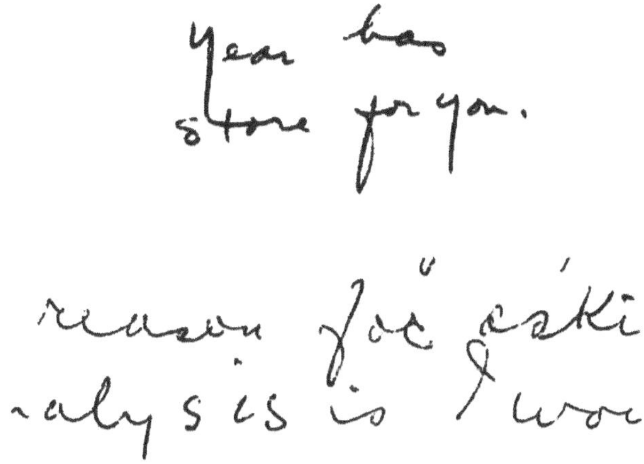

ILLUSTRATION NO. 76

bears out the versatility. The first sample is from a man who does creative work in the advertising field; the second one is written by a woman who is a secretary in the industrial field, but whose hobby is in philanthropic organizational work.

If a writer consistently uses the conventional letter "s" without ever injecting the printed form, it's generally the sign of the mind that is careful with details.

ILLUSTRATION NO. 77

The letter "t" is mainly significant by the way it is crossed. When the horizontal line is done with the same pressure as the "t" itself, is proportionate in size, and is placed about midway on the vertical stroke, it shows a mind that is careful and usually conventional.

If this same kind of horizontal stroke is much longer in proportion to the "t" it reveals a more self-confident attitude and more individuality in action.

But should this long crossing stroke be made with much heavier pressure than the vertical stroke of the "t" it shows an aggressive personality, and this writer prefers not to be subordinated to anyone else.

The short, heavy-pressure "t" bar reveals a mind that is quick but self-opinionated; this person is impatient for results and is usually stubborn in wanting hings done his way.

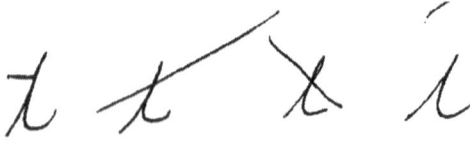

ILLUSTRATION NO. 78

When the "t" bar comes to the letter and stops without crossing through, we know the writer is a procrastinator.

The long crossing stroke which starts low at the left side of the "t" and ascends to a height at the right of it reveals the optimist who aspires to high fulfillment of self, but not necessarily on a material plane.

But the reverse, the stroke which starts high but descends low at the right of the letter, is made by the more cautious individual who is also full of aspirations. The results desired in this case, however, are for material gain as well as recognition from others.

The "t" bar which does not touch the letter, but is flung high above it, shows the person whose imagination works at full speed; there may be high aspirations here, but too many of them belong to the world of day-dreams. Generally these people are enthusiastic about all new ideas, but may not always carry them through.

ILLUSTRATION NO. 79

The amusing "t" crossing of a gracefully curved formation shows the romantic soul, the one who desires gracious living. These writers are usually good hosts and hostesses, rather conventional and hesitant to accept for granted all new trends.

The "t" which does not have a crossing-through bar but is covered at the top with a curved line (like an umbrella) is done by the person who is able to keep the emotions in check. The two ends, curving down, show they are a "cover up" for what may originally have been a more uncontrolled attitude.

But look at the reverse of this, where the "t" is topped by a curved line with the two ends pointing upwards. This person is imaginative, sensitive, and easily affected by surroundings and people, especially if the latter have more dominant personalities than the writer.

The "t" which is tied-up in a knot, rather than being crossed with a separate stroke, is indicative of the person who is able to concentrate on a definite purpose and is persistent once a new plan is undertaken.

At the end of a word the "t" may have a short upward stroke toward the right. This is considered a "t" crossing. It is a conventional formation, but is commonly used by even the most modern thinkers, and shows the practical ability to get down to facts.

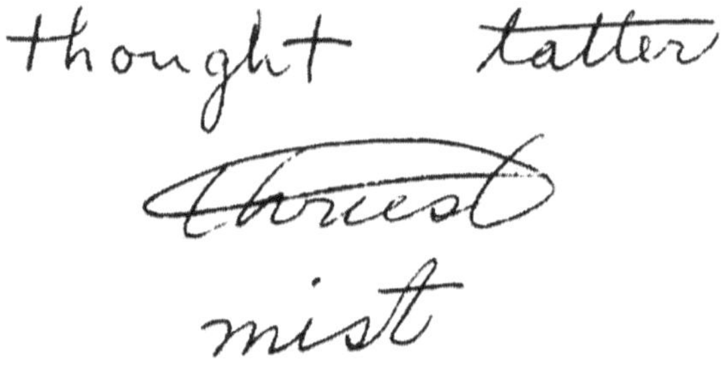

ILLUSTRATION NO. 80

The "t" made with one vertical line then crossed through with a horizontal line, making it a printed formation, often appears in a cursive handwriting. Sometimes it is joined to the next letter by its crossing stroke. This style of "t" crossing is used by people who are usually resourceful in adapting to new ideas, who are not scared of listening to and trying out something that is different. It is often found in the handwritings of people who do creative work.

In a word containing two or more "t's" there may be just one crossing stroke which goes through the multiple "t's" as in the word "tatter" in illustration No. 80. This, of course, shows the writer to be a quick and resourceful thinker as he is able to attain three results with one operation, rather than to need to go through the slower and more cautious process of making three "t" bars in three separate operations.

The "t" which looks like a lasso that goes back and gets itself tied-up (as shown in the word "thrust") is a sign of a tenacious person who holds on to his own opinions.

The one exception, where the letter "t" and not its crossing stroke is of significance, is the "straddle t" formation as shown in the word "mist." This letter usually appears in the handwriting of the person who also makes the "straddle d" mentioned earlier in this chapter, and it has the same meaning. This writer does not betray confidences, is tactful, and shows consideration of other people.

There seems to be no end to the variety of "t" crossings, and when an unusual one shows up in a handwriting the graphologist has to give it individual study and then relate it to the other signs.

When a person makes all sorts of "t" bars, they must be examined very carefully to see which are more dominant and which are rarely done. It is not uncommon to find in the "t" bars in one writing some which show weakness, others reveal strength or sensitivity or aggressiveness — all of different meaning — and it is then that the professional graphologist must weigh one against the other until the seeming contradictions are accounted for in the final analysis.

The "t" is sometimes left uncrossed. If it occurs just once in a specimen of writing which has all other "t's" crossed, then it may just be a temporary slip of the mind or pen. But if a writer shows a chronic tendency not to cross the "t" it may show either a lack of concentration or of regard for details, or it may indicate a poor memory.

More information is given regarding formation of small letters in the next two chapters which deal with beginning and ending strokes, also with letters which are made with loops.

Chapter 13

BEGINNING AND ENDING STROKES

A child, in the first years of writing, will usually put emphasis on the strokes before beginning the first letter of each word, as well as at the end of the last letter of the word. But as maturity of mind and experience instinctively portrays the development of the person in the handwriting, many of the beginning and ending strokes in an adult's writing are eliminated; the word is written by commencing directly with the letter itself and is usually ended with a short stroke or none at all.

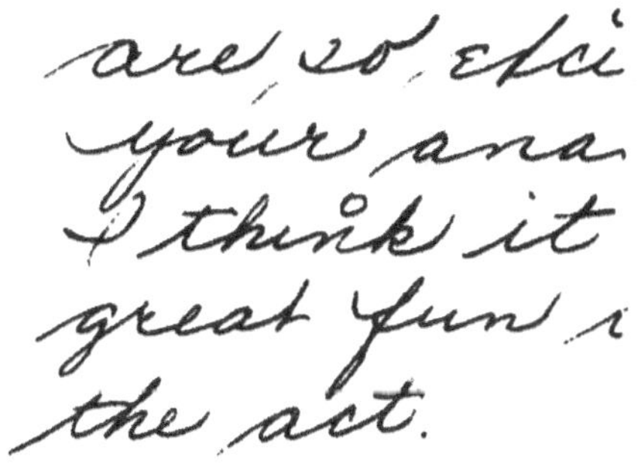

ILLUSTRATION NO. 81

In this sample of writing you see the strokes made at the beginning and ending of the words. They disclose the writer to be conventional, hesitant to rush into any new or unfamiliar plans without first having a chance to work them out carefully in detail. Of course the many other signs of the writing must be taken into consideration in studying these strokes; in a rounded handwriting (as in this illustration) it shows a cooperative spirit and passive acceptance of convention. But if the handwriting is done with angular formations, and still has beginning and ending strokes, it will show the writer to be shrewder and more exacting, although still conventional in attitude.

83

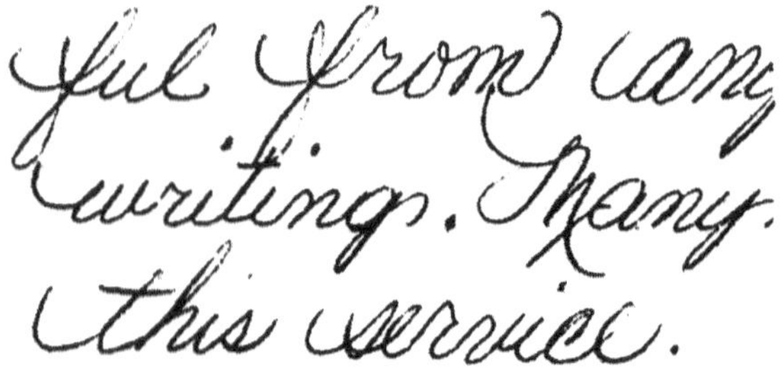

ILLUSTRATION NO. 82

This specimen reveals traits similar to illustration No. 81, but it is shown to call attention to the longer ending strokes which are curved and graceful. The significance of the long, curved ending strokes is congeniality; this person needs social life and likes to work where there are many people.

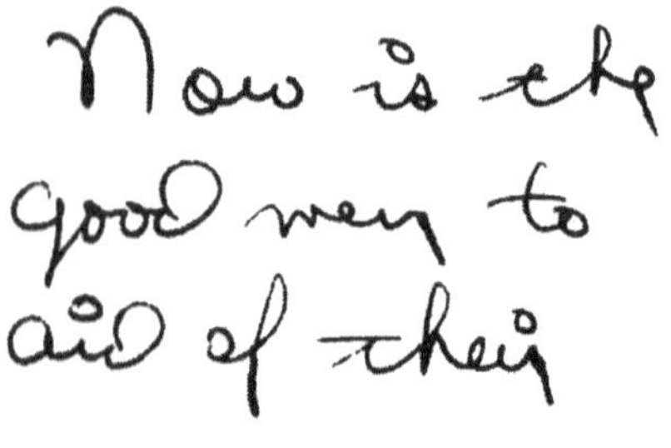

ILLUSTRATION NO. 83

When the last letter ends in a downstroke it reveals a desire to be independent in thought and action; yet the writer might not have other supporting qualities in the handwriting to bear this out. Thus, the downstroke may be stubbornness without ability to carry out all desires. For instance, in illustration No. 83 the writing is naturally rounded even though there are some angular tendencies; so that while this person has some stubborn ideas (shown in the ending strokes coming downward) it is doubtful if they are always put into motion or carried through to a result.

In an angular handwriting the downward thrust of the ending stroke usually reveals definite opinions, not easily swayed or affected by what others say and do.

When the downstroke at end of word is written with very heavy pressure, sometimes looking like a blunt stroke, the opinionated attitude is more exaggerated. These writers must have their own way in all matters.

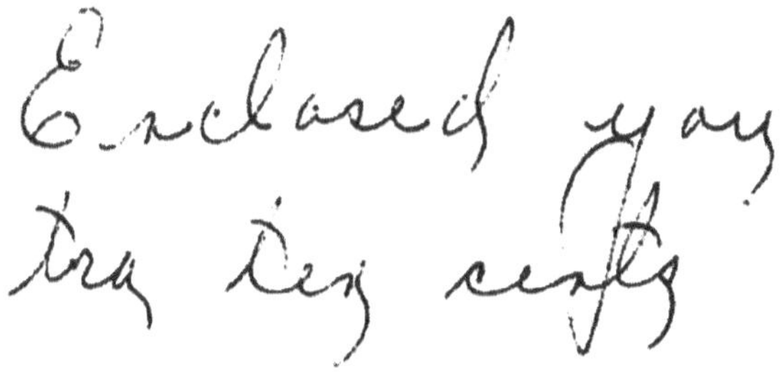

ILLUSTRATION NO. 84

Here is an amusing version of the ending stroke which is written downward. While stubbornness is shown here, it is a flexible matter; this writer usually ends up doing the conventional thing and conforming to what everyone else does. And this is also borne out in the beginning strokes made on the letter "y" and the V.

ILLUSTRATION NO. 85

The exaggerated long ending stroke in Shaw's signature clearly points to his being self-opinionated. It also shows a good deal of intellectual courage and leaves no doubt of his outstanding personality. The closely-connected letters and the restraint in the way they are spaced show his logical, careful mind; yet the ending stroke is a giveaway of his desire to be noticed and acclaimed. Any person who makes such an obviously large ending stroke is making a bid for applause.

ILLUSTRATION NO. 86

The long, straight ending stroke is a sign of the writer's self-confidence. The degree of this trait has to be studied in its relation to the various other indications in the sample of handwriting. In the specimen shown here the writing is angular and the pressure heavy, and so we see that the self-confidence is backed by mental and physical vitality.

If the writing is rounded and light in pressure, and it contains the long ending strokes, it shows the person has confidence in self but not in such a domineering way as the one who writes angularly and with heavy strokes.

Some people do not make beginning or ending strokes on the words they write, and some use one but not the other. Illustration No. 86 has no beginning strokes yet the words certainly have ending strokes. This, then, reveals that the writer is not hesitant at first in going ahead with a new idea and breaking away from convention; nevertheless, the ending stroke shows there is the tendency to hold on to own opinions.

When the words do not have either beginning or ending strokes, the writer is able to concentrate on what is to be done, without fussing over non-essentials either before or after the task. Should a handwriting of this sort (without strokes at beginning or ending words) have distinctive signs of a highly developed intellectual quality, the writer, besides the ability to concentrate and work efficiently, also has the ability to construct new ideas and develop ways to work them out.

We now come to another way in which the beginnings or endings of letters are treated by some writers, and that is the "hook" which may be large or small. In the latter case you may need a magnifying glass to verify that they are hooks rather than ink blobs resulting from a faulty pen. Sometimes the hooks appear on the "t' crossing strokes and on capital letters, in addition to or rather than on beginning and ending strokes of the words.

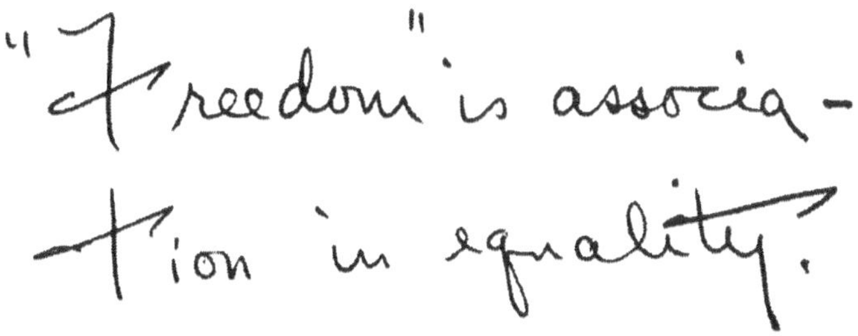

ILLUSTRATION NO. 87

In this sample hooks are shown on the "t" bars. The hook shows tenacity, a "hanging on" to an opinion, or perseverance once a task is started.

You may sometimes see a handwriting where the little hooks appear only at the beginning of the word and not at the end of its last letter, or only at the start of the "t" bar and not at its end. In such case, the writer may be stubborn to start out with, but usually ends up by being willing to see the other person's point of view, and much of the tenacious attitude is relaxed.

However, should the hooks appear only at the end of the "t" bar or only at the end of the word (as shown in illustration No. 86) the reverse may hold true. The writer may proceed with a new plan in an open-minded and cooperative attitude toward the other person's ideas, but after the project is in motion may feel that his own opinions are better and will then tenaciously hold on to them and not be so receptive to the ideas of others.

Should the hooks be seen both at the beginning and ending of the word or the "t" bar, they reveal the person who is naturally persistent even before he starts something new, and this attitude is sustained throughout his activities, and remains to the very end of what he aims to achieve.

In a general sense we find more hooks in a writing of small size because the person who writes small is concerned with details; also in handwriting that is angular, as the mind is critical and won't race ahead until it accounts for each fact and detail. Of course some large and rounded handwritings have hooks; but then the tenacity is not so great and generally more flexible than in the small and angular scripts.

Chapter 14

THREE ZONES AND LOOPS

A handwriting has some formations which reach above the base line, such as the " l " and "h" and upper part of "f" and other letters. Such letters belong to the "upper zone" of the writing.

Formations which descend below the base line, such as the "g" and "y" and the lower part of "f" and other letters, are called the "lower zone."

The letters which do not have any formations that reach above or go below the base line are commonly known as the "middle zone."

Some handwritings are balanced proportionately in the three zones; in some cases the upper zone may be exaggerated, in others the lower zone may be more emphasized, and in some instances the middle zone may be disproportionately larger than the upper and lower zones. Therefore, the whole sheet of writing should be studied (rather than just the words by themselves) to get the true picture of the three zones of writing and their relationship to one another.

This theory of the three zones is a fairly new development in the science of graphology; it was formulated about thirty years ago by Max Pulver of Switzerland, and it is considered by handwriting analysts as a most worthy addition to the study of personality traits.

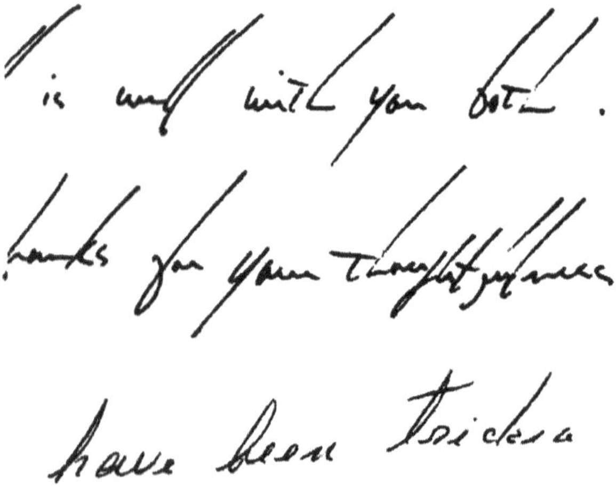

ILLUSTRATION NO. 88

In these two different handwritings you will see that the upper zone is too high in proportion to the middle zone and especially to the lower zone. Notice in the first specimen the letter "f" which is written twice; the half of the letter which goes below the base line is much shorter than its other half which rises high into the upper zone. To interpret this, the upper zone is the intellect, the person's conscious mental desires and aspirations which are not usually based on materialism. This upper zone may also show a spiritual sense (perhaps religion or philosophy). Of course this may not mean precisely the same thing in each handwriting which has a developed upper zone, as the final analysis must be made in its relationship with other signs such as size, pressure and so forth.

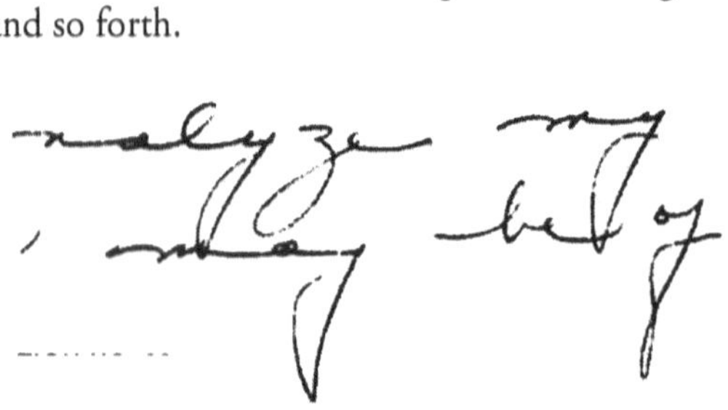

ILLUSTRATION NO. 89

90

When the lower loops of the letters are out of proportion to the letters in the upper and middle zones, the reverse of the foregoing is seen in the picture of the personality. The over-developed lower zone depicts the unconscious emotional and instinctive urges and motivations of the writer; the desire is for self-gratification, for the pleasures of life. Such writers may often talk about their "idealism," but in reality they aim for material comforts and not for self-sacrificing ideals. The graphologist must carefully examine all other signs in the handwriting to see toward which goal the desires are projected.

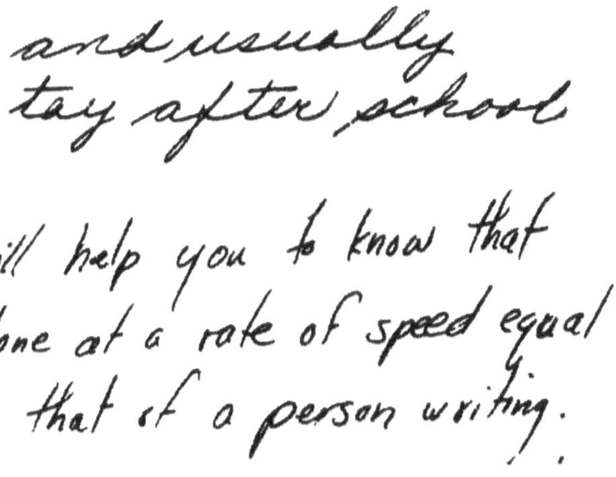

and usually
tay after school

ill help you to know that
one at a rate of speed equal
that of a person writing.

ILLUSTRATION NO. 90

The middle zone is interpreted as the reality of the functioning of the writer in everyday living, the relationship with other people in daily social and working life, the conscious likes and dislikes, the habits developed by the person. A good proportion of all three zones is seen in the specimens of the cursive and manuscript (printed) writing. Neither one of the zones is developed larger or smaller than the others, so the analysis of the handwriting may start off on the premise that this person has a good balance between reality in everyday functioning and the imagination which is held in control, and the emotions are also kept well in check.

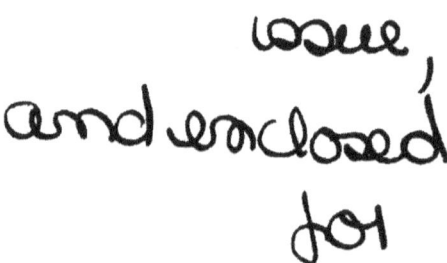

ILLUSTRATION NO. 91

In this specimen the middle zone is over-developed; note the word "enclosed" where the "l" is almost as low as the middle-zone letters, and in the last word "for" the "F" hardly goes below into the lower zone. In such a script the writer has much self-concern, is sentimental rather than realistic in the balancing of the mind and emotions and the daily functioning of her life. Each daily occurrence may assume importance which is not really essential, and that may be because of the lack of imagination (usually found in the upper zone if it's well developed), as well as the lack of motivating physical drive (usually seen in the developed lower zone).

Now that we recognize the general differences in letter formations of the upper, lower and middle zones, we go to more detailed meanings of the individual letters which have loops either below or above the base line, or like the "F" which has both. Usually we find wide loops on letters in a rounded handwriting, as shown in illustration No. 92, and narrow loops (or absence of them) in angular writing such as the two different samples No. 93. But, as is the case with all general rules, there are specific cases where they may not apply in similar manner, especially in the manuscript style of penmanship where the child may not be taught to make looped letter formations. The following information, therefore, bears mainly on the cursive style of handwriting.

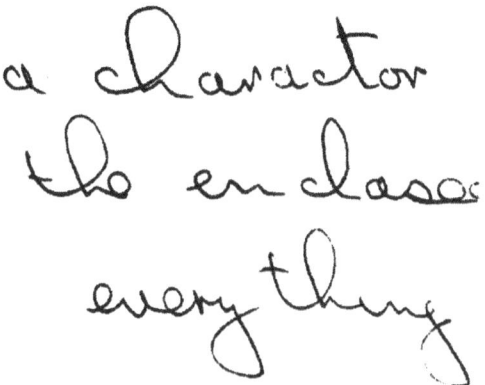

ILLUSTRATION NO. 92

Aside from their meanings because of their placement in upper and lower zones (as explained previously in this chapter) the inflated loops above and below the base line in sample No. 92 are an exaggeration of their "zone" definitions. The overblown upper loops in "h" and "T" show a vivid imagination, and the aspirations may be more for personal satisfaction than for purely spiritual gain. Also, the inflated lower loops in "y" and "g" emphasize the gaiety, the desire for social activities, and a distaste for anything that is confining. This person likes to have nice things, and the ever-young vital personality is usually attractive to others.

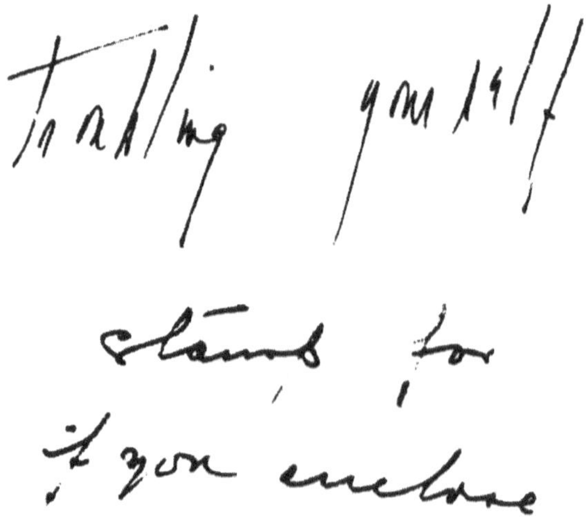

ILLUSTRATION NO. 93

When the loops are absent and the vertical parts of the letters (such as "b", "l", "g", "y" and "f") are made with straight lines, the writing shows the mind's ability to get down to essentials and to work out all plans in a critical manner. Self-confidence is also indicated in the elimination of non-essential loops of these letters. But the degree of that confidence needs to be studied in relationship to other signs in the writing, as well as to the height or depth of such letters according to the zone (upper or lower) to which each belongs. These writers are usually more independent than the ones who make large loops on their letter formations.

A straight-line lower loop which is very short, and sometimes is done with very heavy pressure that comes down bluntly, is a sign of a definite personality. This writer is not easily swayed by others, and the shorter and blunter the downward stroke the more self-opinionated he is.

When the straight-line lower loop is exaggeratedly long (as seen in the first sample in illustration No. 93) it has to be considered in connection with the way in which the writer makes the bar of the "t" crossing. In this case the "t" bar is very long; this signifies the writer has a dominating character and is persistent in his aims. But if the "t" were crossed with a very short bar it would show an aggressive person who did a lot of wishful thinking but was not sufficiently dominating to follow through.

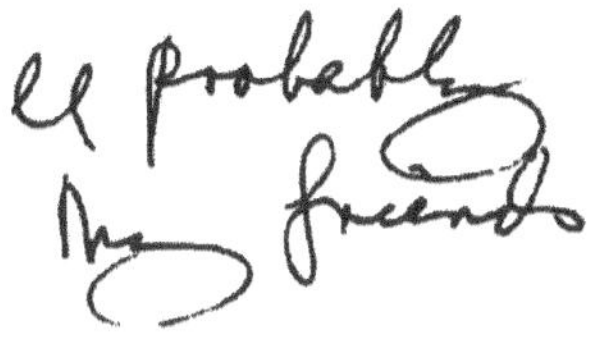

ILLUSTRATION NO. 94

Here you see inflated lower loops, yet the upper ones are proportionately in keeping with the rest of the handwriting. This specimen is to be studied, therefore, as an exaggeration of the lower-zone showing the one who seeks material and emotional pleasures. Yet this attitude does not interfere with the writer's good work and intellect and efficiency.

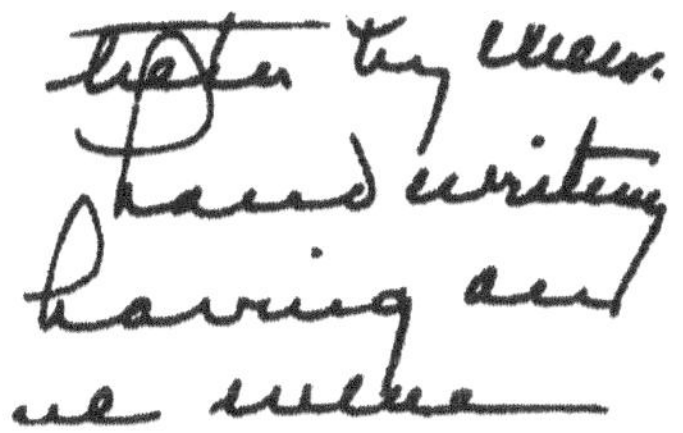

ILLUSTRATION NO. 95

The opposite is shown in this handwriting, where the upper loops are inflated, but the lower ones show the same significance as the ones mentioned in illustration No. 93. Here, too, the writing must be studied according to its upper-zone meaning, and the seeming contradiction of the lower zone has to be related to the rest of the signs in the handwriting. In this case the writer tends to over-emphasize the high aspirations until they become emotional and not just spiritual; yet the ability to "keep the feet on the ground" is also shown, and the combination becomes very interesting.

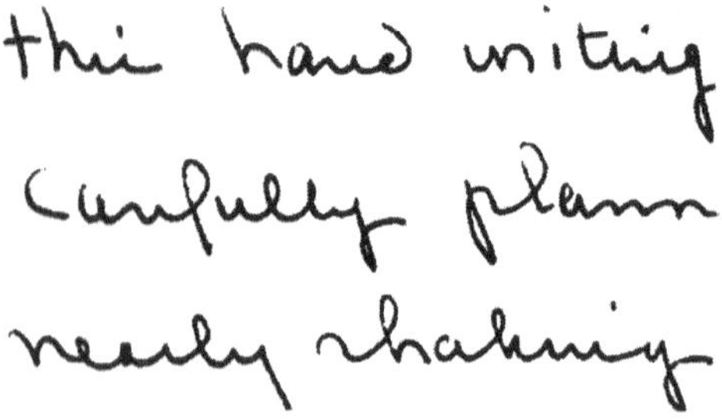

ILLUSTRATION NO. 96

In this specimen we find a good balance between the upper, middle and lower zones, showing that inner conflicts between mind and emotions do not exist, and that the writer is usually able to resolve all problems with clear thinking. However, this writing is shown as an example which contains both loops and straight lines on some of the vertical letters. This, then, signifies the ability to remove non-essentials and get down to fundamentals in thinking, and at the same time it reveals practicality in working out the plans once they are developed in the mind. The analysis, in a case of this sort, is based not only on the loops of the letters, or only on the elimination of the loops; but a complete study has to be made of both kinds of formations in the one handwriting before the result may be obtained. If the handwriting were illegible, or the spaces and pressure and other signs in the writing were erratically changeable, then the combination of both looped and un-looped letters might point to inconsistency. But in the sample shown here the well-balanced three zones, and the other signs in the writing done in an even, rhythmic manner, show a consistent person; the two styles of forming "y" and "h" and other such letters are not a contradiction of one another but are a combination of very sound traits.

ILLUSTRATION NO. 97

96

Sometimes the lower loops are reversed; instead of the loop in the "f" continuing upward to the right it goes to the left and then through the letter, and in the "y" and "g" instead of the loop continuing to the left and through the letter, it turns around and goes to the right and up. The "g" looks like a "q" in some cases. Graphologists usually call these the "altruistic loops." They show that the writer has a maturely intelligent understanding of and interest in other people. The degree of the altruism of understanding or of financial help to others cannot be said to be the same in the case of every writer who makes these "altruistic loops." That trait has to be carefully measured against other determining signs in the handwriting to make sure whether they point to generosity or thrift.

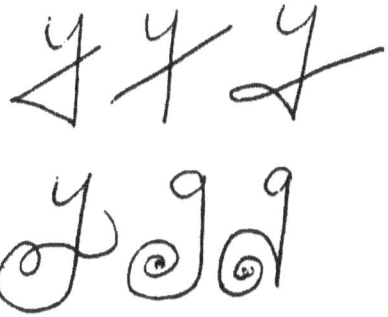

ILLUSTRATION NO. 98

Here are some variations which are seen in lower loops. When they are made in a shut or open angular formation, and appear in an angular handwriting, they are regarded as an emphasis of the critical and persistent traits shown in the writing.

But if the angular loops are made in an otherwise rounded handwriting, they disclose the ability to show determination when needed, although the rounded formations of the rest of the writing prove the persistence or determination is not as strongly basic as in the one who writes with angular formations.

The knot on the angular loop is an emphasis of the writer's tenacity; he may be a stubborn person and hard to convince once his mind is made up in a certain direction.

The little tied-in knot in a rounded loop belongs to the person who might be stubborn at first, yet is not as hard to convince as the one who writes with angular loops. This writer often is hesitant to proceed with a new plan or to accept the other fellow's new ideas, and he deters his planning and action by going back to old methods.

When you see the lower loop decorated with fancy curlicues (as suggested in the two "gs" in the illustration) it is usually a sign of a highly original imagination which may conjure up ideas that have little in common with convention or with practical usage. Such writers are often considered "different" by their friends, and they may have some mild eccentricities of thought or behavior. However, the graphologist may not be able to pinpoint just what they are, so that the "decorated" loops are a puzzling factor and should not be analyzed on their own but studied in their relationship to the other signs in the script.

A sample of handwriting may show variations of the upper and lower loops in one sentence, or even in one word. This is a sign of a many-faceted nature; it may be inconsistency, moodiness or versatility. The handwriting analyst, therefore, must be careful in examining a script in which all sorts of loops are used.

Chapter 15

CAPITAL LETTERS

Usually the capital letter follows the same general style and pressure and is in proportion to the height and width of the small letters in the handwriting. But in some writings the capital letters are conspicuous by their unusual style or their being much taller or wider (or in some cases even smaller) than the small letter formations.

In a cursive handwriting the graphologist often finds printed or semi-printed capital letters; this is an indication of a mind that is constructive, that doesn't become cluttered with non-essential details, and is able to work in a resourceful manner with new ideas.

ILLUSTRATION NO. 99

The semi-printed, simple capitals in the name of Sinclair Lewis reveal his original ideas and his ability to put them to constructive use. You will notice the capital letters are large in proportion to the small ones, and in this case they show pride and self-confidence. Yet this is not to be mistaken for sheer vanity, as the pride of Mr. Lewis was in his work.

ILLUSTRATION NO. 100

Errol Flynn's capital letters are taller than the "l" in his writing, and they reveal high aspirations (ascending high into the upper zone). But in contradiction to his reputation as the perpetual playboy, the capital "E" starts off with a strong stroke knotted at top, and the end of the letter closes with a knot; the "F" ends with a blunt hook. These are signs of persistence, hard work toward a definite goal: they signify pride and aspiration for personal achievement rather than to be a conforming "one of the group" sort of worker.

While in both cases they used large and attractive capital letters, showing pride and aspiration, the difference in these capitals is that in the case of Mr. Lewis he relied on his intuition and imagination, while Mr. Flynn was the critical perfectionist in his work (this is also borne out in his small letters).

Inflated capital letters show the writer wants to be noticed. If, in addition, the capitals are over-ornamented, it's a sign of vanity; these writers like to meet others (else, how could they be noticed?) and are sociable people. Also they are conventional and don't rush into all new ideas.

ILLUSTRATION NO. 101

Here is the comparison between fancy capitals and the unadorned modem styles. The latter show a more direct and sophisticated approach to people and ideas.

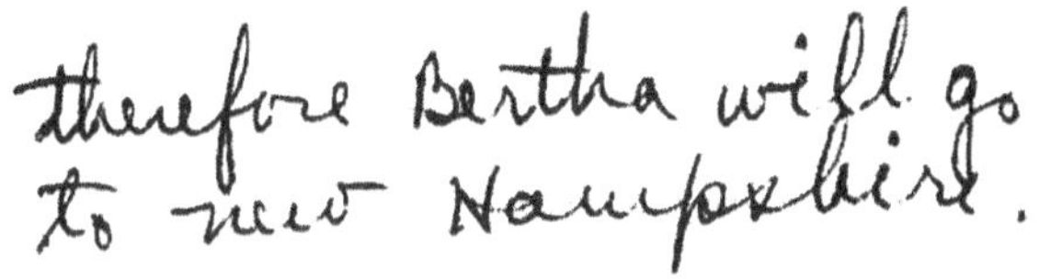

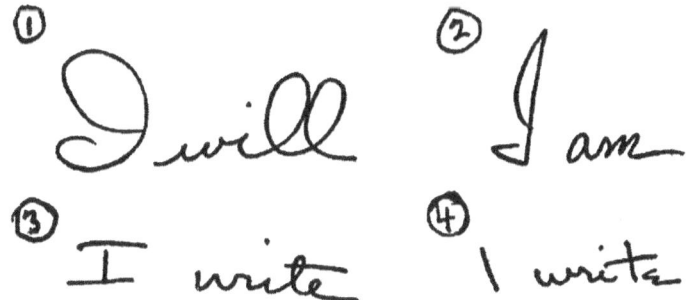

ILLUSTRATION NO. 102

Capital letters which are short in proportion to the size of the small letters disclose lack of self-assertiveness. Such a writer might show his keen intelligence and efficiency by the small formations he makes, yet the under-sized capitals are the sign of his hesitancy to proceed with sufficient confidence. The capital "B" in "Bertha" and the small "N" and "H" in "New Hampshire" conspicuously fail to reach into the upper zone where they belong.

The foregoing information on capital letters is of general interest and applies to the twenty-six capitals in the alphabet. But there are some specific letters which bear studying; this is especially true of the capital "I" and many variations are shown here:

ILLUSTRATION NO. 103

1.   Personal vanity is seen in the inflated "I" especially if accompanied by large loops in the other letters.

101

2.   The angular "I" shows a sense of fairness, a reserved manner. Pride of the clan is seen in this capital, but no personal conceit.

3.   The printed "I" in a cursive writing discloses pride of accomplishment; it is a sign of cool self-confidence.

4.   Generally this has the same meaning as the pre ceding "I" but here there is more reserve; good taste and intellectual quality of mind are also shown.

ILLUSTRATION NO. 104

5.   While this "I" is rather tall in proportion to the small letters, it is not exaggeratedly over-sized. It shows friendliness, also self-confidence but not vanity.

6.   The angular "I" discloses a critical attitude, a desire to work with a definite purpose.

7.   The inconspicuous capital shows there is no pre tense in the person's make-up; it is the sign of a cooper ative spirit.

8.   When the "I" in a forward-leaning handwriting is pulled back, it reveals a lack of aggressiveness.

102

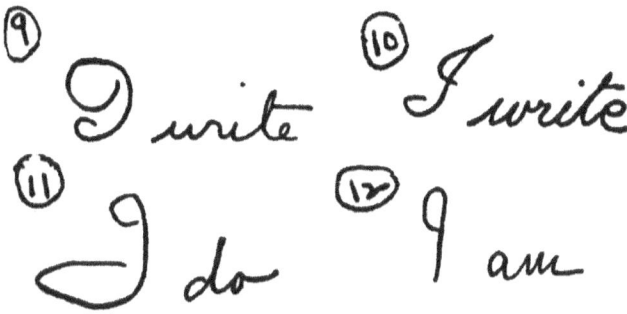

ILLUSTRATION NO. 105

9.   This looks like a squatty "Q" and it shows a rather conventional person, who adapts congenially to social life. He likes to be noticed, yet the desire is prompted by a sense of humor rather than vanity.

10.   This is an old-fashioned "I" which reveals tact in dealing with people. The impulses are held in check and the manner is reserved.

11.   The inflated lower part of the "I" reveals pride, a sense of responsibility, and a serious attitude.

12.   This indicates good taste, discipline of emotions, and pride without conceit.

ILLUSTRATION NO. 106

The "A" which is done in this old-fashioned manner is the "protective A" which reveals a desire to aid those in need; this writer is glad to work cooperatively with others.

The capital "D" which is written so that the stroke comes back into the letter is a sign of the introvert.

ILLUSTRATION NO. 107

1. The incurve at the beginning of the "M" reveals the clannish instinct, cooperative spirit, and the tendency to follow conventional lines of thought and action.

2. But the angular incurve, while it also indicates clannishness, reveals much less cooperative action. This person is critical, and usually proceeds in an aggressive manner to attain desired results.

3. The beginning curve, flung outward, discloses the individual who is sociable, wants to meet people and have fun, likes to defy convention but may not always do so because of cautiousness.

4. The "M" whose first loop (arcade or point) is higher than the other two shows the person who wants success, is not easily discouraged, and takes great pride in per sonal achievements.

5. When the second loop or point is higher than the first or third ones, it's a sign that the writer is very much concerned with his own self; has many original and often unusual ideas which may not be shared with others. This personality is not easily understood.

6. The "M" with the third loop or point higher than the preceding ones is indeed difficult to comprehend by others. The professional handwriting analyst studies this kind of

writing very closely to find other clues which will lead to or fit in with this capital "M." It is usually a sign of stubbornness, of a desire to carry out his own ideas without first divulging them to others.

Whatever is said about the "M" also applies to the capital "N" and it is analyzed in the same way.

If in a specimen of handwriting the same capital letter appears in many different forms, the graphologist determines (through examination of other signs in the writing) if the variations are due to inconsistency, versatility, lack of concentration, or whatever else may be found as the explanation for the different styles of one capital.

Chapter 16

SIGNATURES

While a signature is interesting to the graphologist, it is not preferable by itself as a subject for analysis; it should be accompanied by some lines of handwriting. The reason for this is that often a signature is different from the body of the writing; some people consciously devise a special kind of signature for signing checks, and some have two different ways of signing their names (one for personal letters, another for their business papers).

A graphologist often receives a request for an analysis of a signature placed at the end of a typewritten business letter; in this case extra caution has to be used to ascertain who signed the letter because the name may have been signed by a secretary rather than by the one who actually dictated the letter. (It is not an uncommon procedure for a busy executive to delegate this chore to his secretary.)

The signature is the "outer personality" and when it shows marked differences from the handwriting it is a deliberate wish to impress others in a certain way. So let us see how the facades, created by signatures, are a cover-up for the inner personality:

When the name is written with backhand (to the left) formations, but the handwriting itself is forward-leaning (to the right), the outer personality is cool and reserved and does not reflect the real warmth and friendliness of the character.

But when the signature is written with forward-leaning strokes to the right, and the body of the handwriting is backhand, the outer personality is much warmer and friendlier than the writer really is. The backhand writing shows reserve and concern with self, rather than the outgoing friendliness as the forward-leaning signature tries to impress upon others. You may find this to be the case in the handwriting of many people in public life, who find it necessary to project a warm attitude outwardly yet who may be naturally reserved. This doesn't mean that it is always a deliberate deception; but it does show the person is aware of his obligations to the public and tactfully he plays the role expected of him.

A signature with very heavy pressure in a handwriting done with light pressure is also a contradiction; the outer personality appears aggressive, yet the inner character is sensitive and not self-assertive.

Reversely, if the signature is done with a light pressure and the handwriting is heavily written, the inner person is aggressive but he puts on an outer personality of sensitivity and meekness.

Size differences are also interesting; if the signature is written very large in proportion to the small size of the handwriting itself, it's a sign of an assumed expansive and gregarious outer personality; but the small writing portrays the inner character which belongs to the person who is more interested in working with facts and details rather than dealing with people on a wide scale.

When the signature is very small in proportion to the large size of the handwriting, the outer personality presents a reticence which really doesn't exist. The large formations of the writing itself indicate an outgoing nature and desire to meet people.

A signature composed of angular formations and narrow spaces between the letters, when found in a handwriting that is rounded and has wide spaces, reveals the outer personality is purposely built-up to present a critical and self-sufficient attitude. Yet the rounded writing shows that underneath this cold exterior lies a heart that is warm and affectionate.

When the opposite is seen (where the signature is done with rounded formations and wide spaces, but the writing itself is angular and the spaces are narrow between letters and words) the outer personality is friendly and charming; but it is a cover-up for the innate character which is critical and restrained, and no ideas or people are accepted unless the mind approves.

Occasionally a period is placed at the end of a signature. This is not called for in rules of punctuation, so that putting the small dot (or sometimes artistic people use the small circles) after the signature shows the action to be deliberate. After a while this becomes an unconscious writing gesture. In some cases the period means defiance or self-sufficiency, in others it signifies caution, or it may show a meticulous mind which leaves no detail undone. The interpretation of the period, to know in which of these categories it belongs, needs to evaluated in conjunction with the many other signs in the handwriting. For instance, in an otherwise aggressive writing the period after the signature shows defiance or self-sufficiency, in a handwriting that portrays efficiency the period is a further emphasis of the desire to achieve perfection in all that is done; and in a writing that otherwise shows reserve and caution the period after the signature is an added indication of extreme caution and a hesitancy to proceed with anything that is unfamiliar to the writer. In illustration No. 108 you will see a period placed after Thackeray's signature which, in this case, is the sign of strict attention to detail.

We now come to a popular question which reaches most graphologists, and that is to tell why people underscore their signatures. Generally, when a person puts a line under his name, he is calling attention to himself. An underscoring is a sign of self-confidence or vanity or a bid for attention in some way; the type and size of the line under the name bears out the degree to which the writer possesses this personality trait.

ILLUSTRATION NO. 108

The simplicity of Lincoln's signature is self-evidence of no attempt to produce an outer facade to impress anybody! He wrote his name in the same way as the rest of his handwriting. There is no underscoring of the signature, no obvious bid for attention.

The straight underscoring in Thackeray's signature shows his self-confidence. The line is unadorned and firm, so that his confidence is based not on vanity but on the knowledge of his ability to think and work with good results.

ILLUSTRATION NO. 109

The signature of Samuel Clemens (who wrote under the name of Mark Twain) is underscored with a short line which has a flourish in it. It is done clearly and quickly, with no attempt to add any curlicues to it. This shows some self-assertiveness, but it is tempered with a sense of humor. There is a bit of justifiable vanity, just enough to give more impetus to his confidence in his work; but not sufficiently evident to label him a vain man.

ILLUSTRATION NO. 109 A

Under the signature of Lord Beaconsfield (England's Benjamin Disraeli) the long, gracefully curving line shows artistic perception, as well as love of recognition, and of course diplomacy!

ILLUSTRATION NO. 110

These two signatures of musical fame (Caruso, the operatic tenor, and Paderewski, the composer-pianist) show underscorings which are similar in their bid for acclaim and applause. They are made with graceful lines which end in artistic adornments. These are no "modest shrinking violets."

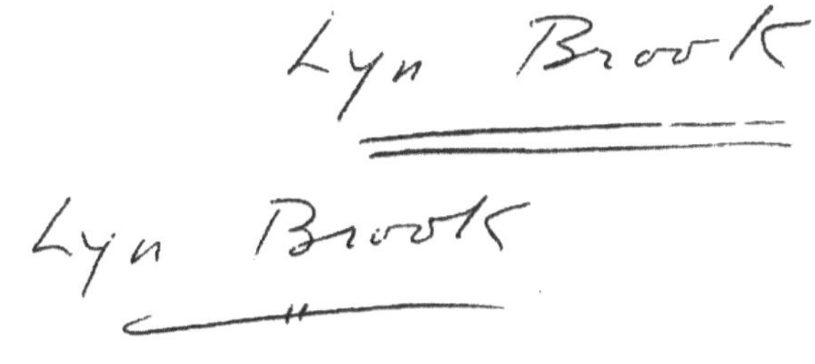

ILLUSTRATION NO. 111

When the signature is underscored with a double line (either straight or curved) it reveals a desire to be the dominant figure in the home or in social or business life. The two little lines (or sometimes dots) placed in the center of the underscoring line is the sign of the person who has the instincts of a trader. In whatever field of endeavor such a writer is, attention is paid to the finances and this individual is not easily fooled in a bargain.

ILLUSTRATION NO. 112

An unconventional manner of signing the name is when an "over-scoring" is added above the signature, rather than an underscoring beneath the name. The type or size of the "over-scoring" line is not important; but what is significant is that the writer has a highly original mind, sometimes eccentric in ideas, and is not easy to understand. But no hasty judgment must be passed upon this unusual signature style; meticulous attention must be given to all the signs in the body of the handwriting to determine the underlying reason for this unusual treatment of the signature.

Just because a signature is not underscored (or has no period after it) does not mean the writer has no self-confidence or vanity or defiance or caution, or whatever it is that the underscore or period signifies. This is mentioned so that you will know it is not essential for a signature to have anything added to it in order to prove the personality strengths or weaknesses.

As a person matures (or perhaps unfortunately retrogresses) the developmental changes may instinctively take place in the signature. (This also applies to the rest of the handwriting, but in this chapter we discuss just the signatures and their meanings.) A case in point is shown in the two signatures of Henry George, the economist and social philosopher.

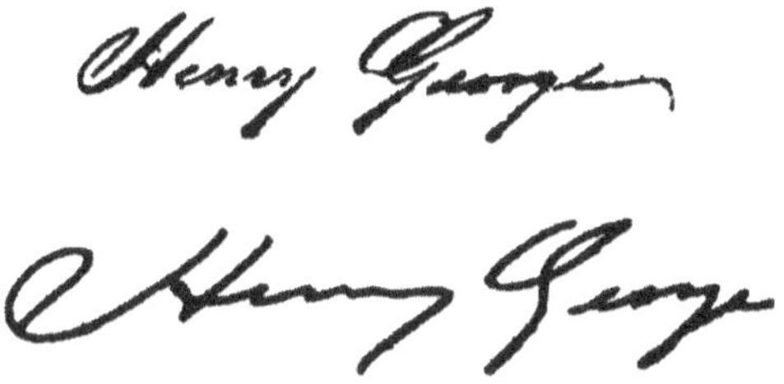

ILLUSTRATION NO. 113

While basically the two names have the same forwardleaning slant (also the proportion of the three zones is not changed, and the style of the capital letters remains the same) you will notice a speedier rhythm of writing and much wider spaces in the bottom signature. In the first signature, written at the age of twenty-two, the formations are deliberate, self-conscious, each letter meticulously formed, and the desire to make good is a very cautious one. But the bottom signature was written at the age of forty-three, and it shows a more courageous, free-flowing style, with all self-consciousness eliminated. A graphologist does not call a case of this sort a "changed" signature; instead, it is recognized as a "development" of innate intellect and a maturity of the sense of values.

Chapter 17

DOODLES

The word "doodle" came into being not too long ago; it describes the scribblings that are made by people while they are telephoning, or perhaps waiting at a desk or table for someone to come along. Or perhaps the person is attending a meeting, and keeps on doodling while the speaker is delivering his oration.

The chronic doodler is not aware of his subconscious action of the hand and the pen or pencil which it holds. The telephone conversation might be about a comedian on a television program, or perhaps giving an order to the butcher, yet the scribbles on the pad may turn out to be something completely different than the subject of the conversation which is consciously going on at the same time. You might be drawing a little house while talking about the comedian, or a bar of music while ordering the lamb chops.

Of course it's not hard to conclude that if a person doodles dollar signs he thinks about money; or if a bar of music or notes or a treble clef is made, then the doodler has a feeling for music. But in many cases the scribbler is puzzled as to why he makes certain doodles which are completely unrelated to the time and place, and the graphologist is often called upon to make an analysis of them. As a rule it is best not to rely on the doodles alone, as the analysis might not be too exact; it is wise to see a few lines of the handwriting and then use the scribblings as a supplement in studying and evaluating the formations of the writing. However, in a general sense, here is the way to find the meanings in the unconsciously drawn scribblings:

ILLUSTRATION NO. 114

Pleasant faces are made by people who are gregarious; they like to meet other people.

But ugly faces indicate a skeptical attitude about people, or may mean that the doodler is in a pessimistic mood.

ILLUSTRATION NO. 115

When maps and directional charts are made, the doodler undoubtedly likes to travel.

Hearts are the sign of the romantic person. And if a little doll is included (or made separately) the desire for a family life is disclosed.

ILLUSTRATION NO. 116

Cottages, cups and saucers, flowers, all show a desire for home life. Often furniture is included in such doodles.

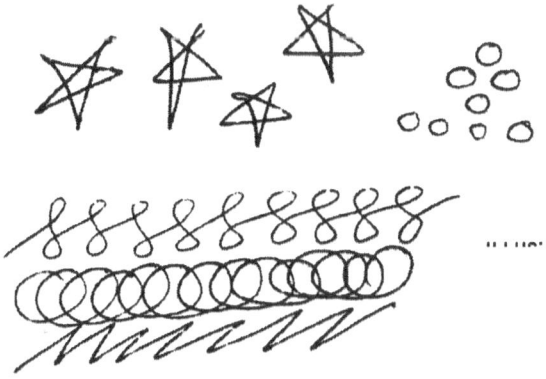

ILLUSTRATION NO. 117

Stars are a sign of optimism, while individual little circles add a spiritual quality to the optimism and faith.

The continuous and repetitious line of one form, such as the "s" and the circle and angled lines, is an indication of the logical mind which is able to clarify an idea.

ILLUSTRATION NO. 118

The doodles which have no definite pattern, but are just a meaningless lot of involved lines of scribbling, disclose the person's worried or unrelaxed train of thought; perhaps there are some unsolved problems.

The filled-in corners and borders of squares and triangles are the sign of the organizer who is capable of good planning.

ILLUSTRATION NO. 119

The geometrical patterns also show the planner, especially the person who likes to analyze existing plans and get down to fundamentals.

ILLUSTRATION NO. 120

Graceful and humorously drawn animals and birds disclose a sense of humor and imagination. They are often found in the scribblings of people who write fiction or give humorous lectures.

Of course there are hundreds of other doodles which individuals make, expressive of their inner personalities; but the foregoing explanations serve as clues to the way in which the analyst views them. Doodles are often referred to as suppressed desires exposing themselves through the pen or the pencil.

Some people never doodle. That may mean that the person does not have any inner conflicts or suppressed desires. But, unless the handwriting and the signature are studied by the graphologist, it is best not to make any superficial statement as to why there is an abstinence from doodling.

In summing up, the INNER YOU is shown in the scribbles you make as well as in the way you write. There is no specific type or group into which the professional graphologist places a doodle or a handwriting. You are distinctly an individual, and every writing formation and scribble that you make is instinctively the gesture of your individual personality.

The purpose of this book is to help you to know your own inner self as well as to understand the personalities of the people with whom you associate in your work, your family, and your social life.

BIBLIOGRAPHY

AUTHOR	BOOK TITLE
Allport and Vernon	Studies of Expressive Movements
Harry C. Brooks	Your Character From Your Handwriting
Hans J. Jacoby	Analysis of Handwriting
J. Crepieux-Jamin	The Psychology of the Movements of Handwriting
Helen King	Your Doodles
DeWitt B. Lucas	Handwriting and Character
Irene Marcuse	Key to Handwriting Analysis
Alfred 0. Mendel	Personality in Handwriting
Max Pulver	Die Symbolik der Handschrift
Henry A. Rand	Graphology — A Handbook
Louise Rice	Character Reading From Handwriting
Klara Roman	Handwriting — A Key to Personality
Dorothy Sara	Handwriting Analysis
Robert Saudek	Psychology of Handwriting, and Experiments with Handwriting
Ulrich Sonneman	Handwriting Analysis
Stein-Lewinson & Zubin	Handwriting Analysis
Frank Victor	Handwriting — A Personality Projection
Werner Wolff	Diagrams of the Unconscious

Sample your own handwriting.

Write DePURA five times below :

Sample your own handwriting.

Write DePURA five times below :